W9-AND-173

Ken Kostick's island Cookbook

What's for Dinner? on Location

MACMILLAN CANADA

TORONTO

Copyright © by Ken Kostick 1997

All rights reserved. The use of any part of this publication reproduced, transmitted in any form or by any means, electronic, mechanical, recording or otherwise, or stored in a retrieval system, without the prior consent of the publisher, is an infringement of the copyright law. In the case of photocopying or other reprographic copying of the material, a licence must be obtained from the Canadian Copyright Licensing Agency before proceeding.

Canadian Cataloguing in Publication Data

Kostick, Ken, 1954–
  Ken Kostick's Island cookbook

Includes index.
ISBN 0–7715–7463–0

1. Cookery, Caribbean.   I. Title.   II. Title: Island cookbook.

TX716.A1K67 1997   641.59729   C96–932482–0

Macmillan Canada wishes to thank the Canada Council, the Ontario Arts Council and the Ontario Ministry of Culture and Communications for supporting its publishing program.

This book is available at special discounts for bulk purchases by your group or organization for sales promotions, premiums, fundraising and seminars. For details, contact: Macmillan Canada Special Sales Department, 29 Birch Avenue, Toronto, Ontario M4W 1E2. Phone: (416) 963-8830.

Macmillan Canada
A Division of Canada Publishing Corporation
Toronto, Canada

1 2 3 4 5 TRI 01 00 99 98 97

Cover and Book Design: Campbell Sheffield Design Inc.
Cover Photo: Jamie Hanson
Photo on p. 1: John Vanderschilden
Composition: IBEX Graphic Communications Inc.

Printed in Canada

I would like to dedicate this book to Jamie, Ruby and Pearl.
Without their support and love none of this would have been possible.

Acknowledgments

Writing a book like this requires a lot of support from friends and colleagues. Without the following people, I could never have accomplished the television show, or this book.

KAREN WOOKEY, producer of What's for Dinner? and close friend: All I can say is thank you and I love ya.

DONALD MARTIN: thank you for being you and giving me the advice I needed over the past year.

NICOLE DE MONTBRUN, my editor at Macmillan Canada: thank you for your guidance and constant encouragement, not to mention your lovely sense of humor.

GILL HUMPHREYS, my next door neighbor (Yes, she really does exist!) who I love and respect: thanks for being a guinea pig and always being honest about my recipes. And thank you for being there.

STEVE WEBB: working with you on the television show, and on the specials, has simply been the best time I have ever had at something called "work."

THE TELEVISION CREW: thanks to everyone who worked on the seasons of What's for Dinner?, as well as on location in the Caribbean.

MACMILLAN CANADA: thanks to everyone, from marketing and publicity to sales, administration and creative, who helped make my first book a success and who gave me much-needed advice for this one.

FRIENDLY KITCHEN COMPANY: thank you Peter, Ira, Mike, Laura, Tania, Sarah, Suzanne, and Drew for the constant support you all showed me during the television series and the writing of this book.

LIFE NETWORK: Sue, Jim, Cindy, Janice, and everyone who gave me the encouragement to pursue television and writing—thanks for this opportunity.

ANNE SMYTH and PAULINE HANSON: for making my job a lot easier.

MY MOTHER, HELEN: for your recipes and ideas for this book. And my sister Diane, whom I'm always trying to marry off. (She's still single, guys!)

MY FRIENDS: Rob, Barry, Brian, Craig, Nancy, Doug, Robert and Brent, who kept a sense of humor and encouraged me with the show and the books.

GREAT NORTH, MY MANAGEMENT COMPANY, AND SHAIN, MY AGENT: I appreciate your positive input and feel you have helped me shape my career. And thanks to Rachel, Dana and Jack.

T-FAL CANADA: thank you for the wonderful cookware used to test the recipes.

METRO KITCHEN: thank you for supplying all the kitchenware for the television show.

Thank you to all of the restaurants who allowed us to film on their premises, as well as to reproduce their recipes for the show and in this book.

And thank you to all the viewers and individuals who buy my books.

TRAVEL ACKNOWLEDGMENTS

I want to thank the following people in the travel industry for helping me with the 3 one-hour specials titled What's for Dinner? on Location, Postcards from the Caribbean, and with this book.

CARLSON WAGONLIT TRAVEL: Jennifer Sloan and her staff for helping arrange the cruise, airfare and especially the coordination of the Celebrity Cruise that I will be doing in the fall of 1997. I am very excited about the prospect of travelling with about 200 Canadians on a culinary cruise, which will include recipe demonstrations and seminars.

ENCORE CRUISES: Vanessa Lee and Roseanna Stollard for helping us to choose the beautiful ship the Century. Both Roseanna and Vanessa worked very hard to ensure that everything went smoothly on the ship and at the ports of call. Thank you for all your hard work.

AIR CANADA: Thank you for supplying the travel arrangements for me and the film crew—and for making our trip comfortable.

CELEBRITY CRUISES and the CENTURY: I want to thank everyone at Celebrity Cruises for having me on board your fabulous ship the Century for a month. I travelled on the Eastern Itinerary, which included San Juan, St. Thomas, St. Martin and Nassau, and then to Ocho Rios, Grand Cayman, Cozumel and Key West on the Western Itinerary. Never before have I experienced such 5-star cuisine or casual elegance on any other line. Everything from the cabins and interior design to the Broadway-style shows, and spa were exceptional. And the wonderful service made me feel that I had a home away from home. Thanks.

Contents

introduction

As you may have already figured out, cooking is something about which I am very passionate, and I'm so thankful for the opportunity to share my passion with you on TV and in my cookbooks.

Quite often I am asked how I come up with the ideas for my recipes. My response is very simple: I follow a few guidelines that I feel are very important when preparing meals today.

- I always choose recipes that feature ingredients you can access *at your local supermarket*. This philosophy has been very well received since most of you don't have the time to shop at specialty stores. I also try to choose ingredients that are healthful.

- I always keep in mind your busy schedules and design recipes that look wonderful, taste delicious, are healthful and, most important, are quick. Most of my recipes can be prepared in about a half hour. There are some that may take a little longer, especially desserts.

- I try to prepare food that is very healthful or that has several healthful or low-fat options—as your letters to me have confirmed, I have a viewership that require varied health options. *You* make the decision as to how you want your meal prepared. (I mean, it's your kitchen, right?) Over the past three years I have been able to lose 60 lbs—and keep them off. Keep in mind that this weight loss was not achieved by diet alone but by healthful eating in combination with an exercise regime. I run almost every day and work out at a gym. At 43 years old, I depend on a good diet and exercise to maintain my hectic schedule.

- My recipes are also designed for you to use what you have in your kitchen. Throughout this book, I encourage you to experiment and use leftovers in creative ways. It's so rewarding to create a dish from scratch, or from leftovers, and to have friends and family pat you on the back and say "What a wonderful meal!"

- Cooking should always be a pleasurable experience so, with that in mind, I've tried to make these recipes easy to follow. I'm always looking for ways to uncomplicate the methods in my recipes so that you can accomplish meals without any difficulty, and in very little time.

The TV Show

What's for Dinner? is going into its third season, and that is very difficult for me to believe. When the third season is completed, I will have taped more than 330 episodes and three one-hour specials shot in the Caribbean.

To give you an idea of what's involved in the production of a show like ours: we tape for six weeks, five shows a day! This is a challenging schedule, but our talented crew, which numbers 65, makes it happen.

I am fortunate to work with someone as talented as Mary Jo Eustace, who not only is an excellent chef, actor, songwriter and singer, but who is also a nice person with whom to work. It is her wacky sense of humor that makes the taping of the shows so enjoyable.

I'm exceedingly blessed to be able to work with producer Karen Wookey, who made every aspect of the show easy and enjoyable. And I attribute much of the success of *What's for Dinner?* to a talented group of individuals that includes directors Dennis Saunders, Steve Wright, Steve Webb and Sue Brophey (I would have loved to have been a fly on the wall, in the control room, when Mary Jo and I were cooking!).

The Friendly Kitchen Company, which produces the TV show (executive producers Peter Williamson and Ira Levy), has given the show, as well as myself, a whole new direction. As an executive producer, I too am now involved creatively on a daily basis.

Postcards from the Caribbean

What's for Dinner? went on location for two weeks on a cruise in the Caribbean, and I have to mention here that I had the *best* time. Never having shot on location before, I didn't realize the enormity of the task. Weather, transportation of equipment and staff, tight scheduling—all and more had to be taken into account.

These two fun but grueling weeks have produced not only three one-hour specials for TV, but also this cookbook *and* a 45-minute video highlighting the cruise, island destinations and great food.

Most of the recipes featured in this cookbook do have an island-flavored theme, but all have been adapted to suit a Canadian kitchen. So get out those pots and pans and make some noise in the kitchen. And enjoy!

—Ken

Sauces and Marinades

Dry Jerk Seasoning

Allspice is a member of the pepper family and it imparts a pleasing spiciness. I use it in my Dry Jerk Seasoning to make the perfect seasoning for chicken, beef, seafood or even vegetables. You can add a little to soups and stews, or a pinch or two to omelettes or scrambled eggs. They will take on a whole new flavor!

1 tbsp	ground allspice
1/2 tbsp	ground nutmeg
1/2 tbsp	cinnamon
1 tsp	garlic powder
1 tsp	onion powder
1 tsp	salt
1 tsp	black pepper
1/2 tsp	cayenne pepper
1/2 tsp	chili powder
1/2 tsp	dried thyme

Combine all ingredients well and place in a jar. The seasoning will last indefinitely.

VARIATION:

◎ REPLACE THE DRIED THYME WITH DRIED BASIL.

Health Option:

◎ LEAVE OUT THE SALT.

Jerk Sauce

In the Caribbean, each island has its own version of hot sauce, which is used in many different ways, from sautéing to marinating. My version of hot sauce can be used to flavor seafood, chicken, beef, vegetables, soups and stews. Use your imagination in your kitchen to add a dash of island spice to your favorite recipe.

4–6	hot peppers (jalapeño or scotch bonnet), depending on taste
3 cloves	garlic, minced
1/2 cup	chopped green onion
1/2 cup	light soy sauce
1/2 cup	lime juice
1/2 cup	olive oil
1/2 cup	white vinegar
1/2 cup	orange juice
1 tsp	ground allspice
1 tsp	ground nutmeg
1 tsp	cinnamon
1 tsp	black pepper
1/2 tsp	dried thyme
1/2 tsp	dried basil

In a food processor blend all the ingredients. In a saucepan gently simmer the jerk sauce for 15 minutes, stirring occasionally. Allow the sauce to cool. Refrigerate in a glass jar. The sauce will keep indefinitely.

VARIATIONS:

- REPLACE THE HOT PEPPERS WITH 1 TSP OF CRUSHED RED PEPPER FLAKES.
- AN ADDITION I OCCASIONALLY USE IS 1 TBSP OF ORANGE RIND.

Low-Fat Option:

- REPLACE THE OLIVE OIL WITH 1 TBSP OF CANOLA OIL AND INCREASE THE ORANGE JUICE TO 1 CUP. THE JERK SAUCE WILL BE SOMEWHAT THINNER AND HAVE A FRUITIER FLAVOR.

Caribbean Chili Sauce

Worcestershire sauce was introduced to Britain by the Romans, who simply called it "garum." It is delightfully spicy due to its anchovy base, and certainly adds zest to my Caribbean Chili Sauce. The sauce is a favorite in my kitchen—I use it with seafood and chicken and add it to soups and stews to make them extra special.

1/4 cup	olive oil
8–10 cloves	garlic, minced
4–6	large onions, finely chopped
1	sweet red pepper, chopped
1/2 tsp	crushed red pepper flakes
1/2 tsp	dried basil
2 cups	crushed stewed tomatoes
1/4 cup	dry red wine
1 tsp	Worcestershire sauce
1/2 tsp	salt
1/2 tsp	black pepper

In a large saucepan heat the olive oil; sauté the garlic and onions for 2–3 minutes, until translucent. Add the red pepper and sauté another 2 minutes. Stir in red pepper flakes, basil, tomatoes, wine, Worcestershire sauce, salt and pepper; bring to a boil. Immediately reduce heat and simmer, uncovered and stirring occasionally, 15 minutes, or until sauce thickens. If too thick, add a small amount of water.

VARIATIONS:

○ REPLACE CRUSHED STEWED TOMATOES WITH 6 CHOPPED PLUM TOMATOES, 1-1/2 CUPS OF WATER AND 1 TSP OF TOMATO PASTE.

○ REPLACE THE SWEET RED PEPPER WITH GREEN, ORANGE OR YELLOW PEPPER.

Low-Fat Option:

○ REPLACE THE OLIVE OIL WITH 1/4 CUP OF APPLE JUICE.

Creole Sauce

Creole cuisine is one of the most exciting combinations of Caribbean, African and Hindu cooking. I use my version to spice up chicken, fish, vegetables and even pasta. On lazy Sunday mornings I do a version of scrambled eggs with Creole sauce and some Parmesan cheese.

2 tbsp	olive oil
1	medium onion, chopped
4 cloves	garlic, minced
1	sweet green pepper, chopped
2 cups	crushed stewed tomatoes
1/2 cup	dry red wine
1/2 cup	water
1/4 cup	chopped fresh parsley
1 tbsp	brown sugar
1 tbsp	Worcestershire sauce
1 tbsp	red wine vinegar
1 tsp	dry mustard
1 tsp	crushed red pepper flakes
1 tsp	tomato paste
1/2 tsp	dried basil

VARIATION:

○ REPLACE RED WINE WITH GRAPE JUICE OR APPLE JUICE.

Low-Fat Option:

○ REPLACE OLIVE OIL WITH 1/4 CUP OF VEGETABLE STOCK.

In a large saucepan heat the olive oil; sauté the onion, garlic and green pepper until onion is translucent. Stir in tomatoes, red wine, water, parsley, brown sugar, Worcestershire sauce, vinegar, dry mustard, red pepper flakes, tomato paste and basil; bring to a boil. Reduce heat and simmer, uncovered and stirring occasionally, about 15 minutes, until the sauce thickens. If too thick, add a little water. Allow to cool. Refrigerate in glass jars. This sauce will keep for about 2 weeks.

Mango and Avocado Sauce

There are more than 2,500 types of mango with a wide variety of appearance, from green to red-gold. But whatever the outside, the inside should be a rich golden yellow and oozing juice. Its distinct flavor, combined with avocado, makes my Mango and Avocado Sauce a real taste treat. Use it with any recipe for grilled seafood and poultry. Experiment by adding curry or cinnamon to this sauce. The change will be subtle and savory.

1 cup	chopped avocado
1 cup	chopped mango
1/2 cup	whipping cream
1/4 cup	dry white wine
1/4 cup	water or apple or pineapple juice
2 tbsp	lemon juice
1/4 tsp	salt
1/4 tsp	black pepper
2 tbsp	whipping cream

In a food processor blend avocado, mango, 1/2 cup cream, wine, water, lemon juice, salt and pepper until smooth. Transfer to a saucepan and bring to a boil. Reduce heat and simmer 2 minutes. Allow to cool. Gently stir in 2 tbsp whipping cream.

VARIATION:

⊚ REPLACE THE MANGO WITH PAPAYA OR KIWIFRUIT.

Low-Fat Option:

⊚ REPLACE WHIPPING CREAM WITH NON-FAT SOUR CREAM. SIMMER ON MEDIUM HEAT, MIXING WELL (DO NOT BOIL).

Chart House Bleu Cheese Dressing

"Bleu" is the generic term for veined cows' milk cheese. The Danish variety, often called Danablu, is semisoft, with a buttery, crumbly texture. It has a rich, strong, quite salty taste, making it ideal for this tangy dressing from the Chart House Restaurant in San Juan, Puerto Rico. It is wonderful on salads with poultry and seafood, but I have even used this sauce on grilled sirloin steak. Experiment!

3/4 cup	sour cream
I tsp	Worcestershire sauce
1/2 tsp	dry mustard
1/2 tsp	black pepper
1/2 tsp	salt
1/2 tsp	garlic powder
I-I/3 cups	mayonnaise
4 oz	blue cheese, crumbled

In a blender blend sour cream, Worcestershire sauce, mustard, pepper, salt and garlic powder for 2 minutes at low speed. Add mayonnaise and blend for 30 seconds at low speed; increase speed to medium and blend for another 2 minutes. Reduce speed to low and, with the motor running, slowly add the blue cheese, blending no longer than 4 minutes. Refrigerate for 24 hours before serving.

Low-Fat Option:

◎ USE LOW-FAT MAYONNAISE.

◎ Recipe from the Chart House Restaurant, San Juan, Puerto Rico.

Homemade Barbecue Sauce with Fresh Island Herbs

Balsamic vinegar is known for its smooth sweet/sour flavor. When made in the traditional way, around Modena in northern Italy, it is aged for at least 15 years. This is a sauce you can use on everyday foods like chicken, fish and beef, and I even add it to pasta sauces and soups. This sauce can also be used as a marinade: stir together 1/2 cup of the sauce and 1/2 cup of red wine. Marinate your poultry, fish or beef a minimum of 2 hours.

2 tbsp	butter
2 cloves	garlic, minced
I	large onion, chopped
I cup	apple juice
1/2 cup	dry red wine
1/4 cup	chopped fresh parsley
1/4 cup	chopped fresh basil
I tbsp	chopped fresh thyme
I tbsp	brown sugar
I tbsp	Worcestershire sauce
I tbsp	balsamic vinegar
I tsp	chili powder
1/2 tsp	mild curry powder (optional)
1/2 tsp	paprika
1/2 tsp	salt
1/2 tsp	black pepper
1/4 tsp	cayenne

VARIATION:

◎ REPLACE THE RED WINE WITH APPLE JUICE. SIMMER 5 MINUTES LONGER TO REDUCE.

Low-Fat Option:

◎ REPLACE THE BUTTER WITH I TBSP OF CANOLA OIL.

Health Option:

◎ REPLACE THE BROWN SUGAR WITH A CALORIE-REDUCED LIQUID SWEETENER.

In a deep medium saucepan melt the butter; sauté the garlic and onion until the onion is translucent, about 2 minutes. Stir in apple juice, red wine, parsley, basil, thyme, brown sugar, Worcestershire sauce, balsamic vinegar, chili powder, curry powder (if using), paprika, salt, pepper and cayenne; bring to a boil. Reduce heat and simmer, uncovered and stirring occasionally, 15 minutes or until it thickens. Allow to cool. Refrigerate in glass jars. Keeps 2 weeks in a refrigerator.

Island Orange-Prune Sauce

Scratch any good wine maker and you'll probably find an excellent wine vinegar maker, like that found in the Rioja region of Spain. And there is no more mellow, rich or full-bodied vinegar than a good red wine vinegar, which I have used to make my Island Orange-Prune Sauce. It complements beef and pork marvelously, or use it as a marinade by diluting it with orange juice.

1 cup	pitted prunes
2 tbsp	lemon juice
1/2 tsp	ground nutmeg
1/4 tsp	ground allspice
1/4 tsp	cinnamon
6	cloves
1 cup	orange juice, pulp included
2 tbsp	orange rind
1/2 cup	red wine vinegar
1/4 cup	brown sugar

In a medium saucepan combine the prunes, lemon juice, nutmeg, allspice, cinnamon and cloves. Cook about 2 minutes on medium heat. Add the orange juice and rind; mix well. Simmer, uncovered, until the liquid has reduced, 12–15 minutes. Discard the cloves. In a blender or food processor blend the sauce until smooth. Return sauce to pot and add the vinegar and brown sugar. Stir over medium heat until blended well.

VARIATION:

◉ REPLACE THE BROWN SUGAR WITH 1/4 CUP OF LIQUID HONEY.

Health Option:

◉ REPLACE THE BROWN SUGAR WITH A CALORIE-REDUCED LIQUID SWEETENER.

Caribbean Fruit Salsa

North Americans have come to think of salsa as an uncooked tomato-based relish in varying degrees of hot, hotter and hottest. The word is actually Mexican for sauce, and it is in that sense that I have created this Caribbean Fruit Salsa. With its tasty mélange of fruit, it is ideal to serve on grilled fish or chicken. You can add whatever fresh fruit you might want to use; just beware of fruit that might discolor, like bananas or apples and some pears, although these fruits can be used if you serve the salsa immediately.

1 cup	chopped pineapple
1 cup	chopped mango
1 cup	chopped papaya
1/2 cup	chopped red onion
1/2 cup	chopped cucumber
1/2 cup	chopped sweet red pepper
1/4 cup	chopped fresh coriander
2 tbsp	chopped jalapeño peppers
1 tbsp	chopped fresh dill
1 tbsp	lemon juice
1 tsp	balsamic vinegar

In a large mixing bowl combine all ingredients and mix well. Refrigerate for 2 hours. Serve over grilled food.

VARIATION:

⊙ REPLACE FRUIT WITH ORANGES, GRAPEFRUIT, KIWIFRUIT, GRAPES OR MELON.

Celery and Fennel Salsa

Fennel was introduced to North America around the seventeenth century from Italy. It has a sweet aniseed flavor and, when combined with celery, makes a wonderful salsa for fish or chicken.

1	fennel bulb, finely chopped
4	celery stalks, finely chopped
1	sweet green pepper, finely chopped
1/2	red onion, finely chopped
2	jalapeño peppers, finely chopped
1 cup	chopped fresh coriander
1/2 cup	chopped fresh mint
2 tbsp	lemon juice
1 tbsp	red wine vinegar
1/2 tsp	salt
1/2 tsp	black pepper

In a mixing bowl combine all ingredients. Refrigerate at least 2 hours before serving.

VARIATION:

⊚ REPLACE FENNEL WITH 1 CUP OF CHOPPED CUCUMBER AND ADD TWO MORE CELERY STALKS.

TIP:

⊚ WHEN SHOPPING FOR YOUR FENNEL BULB, LOOK FOR THOSE THAT ARE WELL ROUNDED. FLAT-BELLIED FENNEL BULBS ARE IMMATURE. THE BULBS SHOULD SHOW NO SIGNS OF BRUISING OR BROKEN LEAVES AND THEY SHOULD LOOK DRY BUT, OF COURSE, NOT DRIED OUT.

Salsa Mexicana

The serrano pepper, which is actually a chile, is one of the more common varieties. Carrot-shaped and green, the serrano is strong, hot, and less juicy than other hot peppers. This simple sauce is based on a wonderful combination of flavors put together by my new friends at Pancho's Backyard Restaurant in Cozumel, Mexico.

3/4 cup	diced white Spanish onion
1	serrano pepper, diced
3/4 cup	diced plum tomatoes
	Juice of 2 limes
1/2 cup	chopped coriander leaves
	Salt and black pepper to taste

In a bowl mix all the ingredients together. Serve with tortilla chips.

VARIATIONS:

⊙ REPLACE THE WHITE SPANISH ONION WITH RED ONION.

⊙ REPLACE THE SERRANO PEPPER WITH OTHER HOT PEPPERS SUCH AS JALAPEÑO OR SCOTCH BONNET PEPPERS.

⊙ *Recipe from Pancho's Backyard Restaurant, Cozumel, Mexico.*

Ken's Mexican Salsa

Coriander is one of those ancient wonders—it is spoken of in the Bible, and coriander seeds were found in the tombs of the pharoahs. In its leaf form, it is sometimes called cilantro, and its taste is reminiscent of anise. You'll love it in my Mexican Salsa, which can be served with tortilla chips, egg dishes, chicken or steak. Try adding a little to soups and stews for a delicate difference.

6	medium tomatoes, finely chopped
2	jalapeño peppers, finely chopped
2 cloves	garlic, minced
1/2	red onion, finely chopped
1/2	sweet green pepper, finely chopped
1 cup	chopped fresh coriander
1/2 cup	chopped fresh dill
2 tbsp	lemon juice
1 tbsp	balsamic vinegar

Combine all ingredients in a large mixing bowl. Mix well. Refrigerate for at least 30 minutes before serving. Keeps for approximately 2 weeks in the refrigerator.

VARIATION:

⊚ REPLACE THE TOMATOES WITH CUCUMBER AND ZUCCHINI.

Low-Fat Option:

⊚ THIS RECIPE IS FAIRLY LOW IN FAT ON ITS OWN!

Honey and Garlic Marinade

Roasted soybeans, combined with wheat and then aged for two years, give us that delightful ancient Chinese invention, soy sauce. I use the more modern Japanese version of light soy sauce for my Honey and Garlic Marinade, and I make it extra special by adding curry and ginger. This marinade is great for seafood, beef and poultry. I have even impressed my dinner guests by using it for baked tofu cubes!

3/4 cup	light soy sauce
1/4 cup	liquid honey
6–8 cloves	garlic, crushed
2 tbsp	lemon juice
1 tbsp	Worcestershire sauce
1 tsp	balsamic vinegar
1/2 tsp	chopped or crushed fresh ginger
1/2 tsp	mild curry powder
1/2 tsp	dried basil

In a blender or food processor combine all ingredients well.

VARIATION:

◉ REPLACE THE SOY SAUCE WITH APPLE JUICE AND REDUCE THE AMOUNT OF HONEY TO 1 TBSP.

Health Option:

◉ REPLACE THE HONEY WITH A CALORIE-REDUCED LIQUID SWEETENER.

TIP:

◉ IF YOU PLAN TO USE THE MARINADE AS A BASTING SAUCE WHILE GRILLING OR BAKING, SET SOME ASIDE BEFORE MARINATING SO THAT YOU AVOID CONTAMINATING YOUR MEAT AND SEAFOOD.

Appetizers

Guacamole

The avocado is a pear-shaped fruit with buttery-yellow flesh, rich in oils (and calories)! Abundant in the West Indies and the southern hemisphere, it is the principal ingredient in that classic specialty of Mexican cooking, guacamole, some variations of which are complexities of spice. This recipe from Pancho's Backyard Restaurant in Cozumel keeps it simple and easy, making it a quick, wonderful accompaniment to dishes as well as on its own with tortilla chips.

1	avocado
	Fresh lime juice to taste
Pinch	salt
Pinch	black pepper

Cut the avocado in half and discard the seed. Spoon the flesh into a small bowl; add the lime juice, salt and pepper. Mash until well blended and no big lumps remain.

Focaccia Fingers

SERVES 4–6

I quite often do this recipe as an appetizer or a lunch because it is healthy and easy to prepare. It is also a good way to use up your vegetables.

1 tbsp	chopped fresh rosemary
2 tbsp	chopped fresh basil
2 tbsp	chopped fresh oregano
4 tbsp	olive oil
2	green zucchini, sliced lengthwise
2	sweet red peppers, sliced diagonally
1	red onion, sliced in 1/2-inch rings
1	medium eggplant, sliced in 1/2-inch rings
	Salt and black pepper to taste
2 tbsp	balsamic vinegar
1 tsp	lemon juice
1	12-inch round focaccia bread
1/2 cup	crumbled goat cheese
1/2 cup	shredded carrots
1 cup	fresh parsley for garnish

VARIATION:

⊚ SUBSTITUTE 6 STALKS OF GRILLED GREEN ONION FOR THE RED ONION.

Low-Fat Options:

⊚ REPLACE FOCACCIA BREAD WITH A LARGE PITA AND PLACE VEGETABLES INSIDE POCKET.

⊚ REPLACE OLIVE OIL WITH CANOLA OIL.

⊚ REPLACE GOAT CHEESE WITH 1 CUP OF GRILLED MUSHROOMS.

In a small bowl combine rosemary, basil and oregano. Lightly brush 2 tbsp of the olive oil on the zucchini, red peppers, red onion and eggplant, and place vegetables on grill. Sprinkle with herb mixture and salt and pepper. Grill vegetables, turning occasionally, about 5 minutes or until grill marks appear. (Turn the onion carefully so that rings do not fall apart.)

In a small bowl combine vinegar, lemon juice and remaining olive oil to make dressing.

Cut the focaccia carefully lengthwise and place the vegetables inside. Sprinkle with the goat cheese and carrots. Drizzle the inside with dressing and then cut into fingerlike sections. Arrange on a platter and garnish with fresh parsley.

Sesame Tofu Cubes

SERVES 4

Tofu is the curd made from the soybean, a powerhouse of nutrition. It has the magic of taking on the flavors around it. This wonderful appetizer is a cacophony of tastes and island fun!

4 cloves	garlic, minced
1	small onion, coarsely chopped
1/2 cup	light soy sauce
1/4 cup	dry white wine
2 tbsp	liquid honey
1/2 tsp	chopped fresh ginger
1/2 tsp	crushed red pepper flakes
1/2 tsp	dried basil
1/2 tsp	black pepper
1 lb	firm tofu, cut into 1/2-inch cubes
2 tbsp	sesame seeds

VARIATION:

◎ REPLACE THE TOFU WITH CHICKEN WINGS OR CHICKEN BREASTS CUT IN CUBES.

Health Option:

◎ USE A CALORIE-REDUCED TOFU.

In a food processor combine the garlic, onion, soy sauce, white wine, honey, ginger, red pepper flakes, basil and black pepper; blend until smooth. Transfer to a shallow bowl and marinate the tofu cubes at least 2 hours.

Line a baking sheet with foil and spray with vegetable cooking spray. Arrange tofu cubes on baking sheet; add the marinade and sprinkle with sesame seeds. Bake at 300°F for 10–12 minutes (or broil for 8–10 minutes) until brown; occasionally turn the cubes while baking and sprinkle with more sesame seeds. Allow the tofu to cool. Pierce cubes with colored toothpicks and arrange on a serving platter. Garnish with colorful fruit.

Chiles Rellenos

SERVES 4–6

This is a great appetizer from Pancho's Backyard in Cozumel.

6	large green chile peppers (such as poblanos), with stems
1/2 cup	shredded mozzarella or mild Cheddar
2	eggs, separated
Pinch	salt
2 tbsp	oil for frying
	Sifted all-purpose flour for coating
	Tomato sauce

Remove skins from the chiles, taking care not to break off the stems. Slit the chiles lengthwise and remove the seeds. Place the cheese inside the peppers; secure the slit and any minor tears with toothpicks. In a bowl beat the egg whites with salt until they hold stiff peaks. In a separate bowl lightly beat the egg yolks; gently fold into the whites. Heat the oil in a large, heavy skillet over medium-high heat. When oil is hot, lightly coat the peppers in flour, dip into the egg mixture and place in the hot oil. Cook until browned on one side, then turn and brown the other side. Transfer to paper towels to drain. If necessary, cook the chiles in batches. In another large, shallow pan heat the tomato sauce until warm. Add the cooked chiles and cook just long enough to heat through. Serve immediately with boiled rice.

Low-Fat Option:

⊚ USE A LOW-IN-SATURATED-FATS OIL OR A LIGHTER OIL THAT HAS FEWER CALORIES.

TIP:

⊚ IT'S ALWAYS BEST TO WEAR YOUR KITCHEN RUBBER GLOVES WHEN STEMMING, SEEDING OR CHOPPING RAW CHILE PEPPERS.

⊚ *Recipe from Pancho's Backyard Restaurant, Cozumel, Mexico.*

Baked Jerk Chicken Drumsticks
SERVES 4-6

Garlic tends to stir a dialogue for or against in almost any circle.
Yet love it or hate it, no reputable cook would be without garlic.
It can be purchased in its most common forms, white-skinned,
pink-skinned and purple-skinned, the last choice reputed to be the
best. My Baked Jerk Chicken Drumsticks wouldn't be the same
without the addition of garlic to my jerk spices. You can substitute
chicken breasts or thighs for the drumsticks.

2 lb	chicken drumsticks
	Dry Jerk Seasoning (recipe on page 4)

Arrange the drumsticks on a baking sheet lined with
foil and coat both sides with jerk seasoning. Bake at
350°F for 18–20 minutes, until chicken is no longer
pink inside. Broil for 2 minutes to brown the chicken.

VARIATION:

◉ FOR A VEGETARIAN
MEAL, REPLACE THE
CHICKEN WITH 2
BLOCKS OF FIRM TOFU,
EITHER CUBED OR
SLICED LENGTHWISE.
REDUCE COOKING TIME
TO 10–12 MINUTES.

Low-Fat Option:

◉ REMOVE THE SKIN
FROM THE CHICKEN
DRUMSTICKS.

Chicken Satay in Banana-Peanut Sauce

SERVES 4-6

The banana is a most remarkable food, highly underrated, yet full of carbohydrates, iron and all of the vitamins except D. Here I combine them with nutritious peanuts (which are not nuts at all, but a member of the legume family) for outstanding nutritional value and taste!

4	boneless, skinless chicken breasts, cubed
1	sweet red pepper, cubed
2	bananas

MARINADE

1/2 cup	light soy sauce
1/2 cup	unsweetened coconut milk
1/4 cup	chopped fresh coriander
2 tbsp	peanut oil
1 tsp	brown sugar
1 tsp	balsamic vinegar
1/4 tsp	crushed red pepper flakes
3 cloves	garlic, crushed

BANANA-PEANUT SAUCE

2 cloves	garlic
1	small onion, chopped
1/2	banana
1/2 cup	smooth peanut butter
1/4 cup	pineapple juice
1/4 cup	light soy sauce
1 tbsp	balsamic vinegar
1 tbsp	peanut oil

MARINADE

In a shallow dish combine all ingredients. Set aside 2 tbsp of the marinade for basting.

VARIATION:

◎ USE CUBED SWORDFISH AND FRESH TUNA INSTEAD OF CHICKEN.

Low-Fat Option:

◎ USE LEAN TURKEY BREAST INSTEAD OF CHICKEN.

BANANA-PEANUT SAUCE

In a food processor purée all ingredients until smooth. If the mixture is too thick for dipping, add a little water or more pineapple juice.

Thread chicken and red pepper onto skewers and marinate at least 2 hours in the refrigerator. Grill the chicken skewers 10–12 minutes or until chicken is cooked through, occasionally basting with the reserved marinade to keep the chicken moist. Split the bananas lengthwise and brush with vegetable oil; grill about 2 minutes or until grill marks appear. Place the sauce in a small bowl in the center of a serving dish and arrange the skewers on the plate. Garnish with the grilled bananas.

Grilled Beef Satay with Asparagus and Orange

SERVES 6

Springtime in Spain and *the whiff of orange blossoms* conjures visions of *that* round, plump, juicy citrus, the orange. Its delightful fresh taste combines exquisitely with beef for a light and flavorful island appetizer.

1 cup	orange juice, pulp included
1/2 cup	light soy sauce
1/4 cup	finely chopped chives
2 cloves	garlic, crushed
2 tbsp	orange rind
1 tbsp	chopped fresh mint
1 tbsp	Worcestershire sauce
1 tsp	brown sugar
1/2 tsp	crushed fresh ginger
1 lb	top round, cut into 1/2-inch cubes
3	large oranges, cut into 12 wedges
6	thick asparagus spears, halved crosswise

In a bowl combine the orange juice, soy sauce, chives, garlic, 1 tbsp of the orange rind, mint, Worcestershire sauce, brown sugar and the ginger. Set aside 1/4 cup for basting. Thread the beef, orange and asparagus onto the skewers and marinate for at least 2 hours in the refrigerator. Grill skewers until beef is medium rare, 6–8 minutes, occasionally turning to get grill marks and basting with reserved marinade. Sprinkle with remaining orange rind.

VARIATIONS:

◎ REPLACE ORANGES AND JUICE WITH GRAPEFRUIT.

◎ REPLACE THE SUGAR WITH 1 TBSP OF ORANGE LIQUEUR.

Low-Fat Option:

◎ REPLACE BEEF WITH TURKEY OR SWORDFISH.

Calamari in Lemon Tomato Sauce
SERVES 4–6

In the Caribbean the combination of spices and citrus dates back to the first settlers. In this recipe I use a spicy tomato sauce with the calamari and wake up the taste buds with the lemon.

2 tbsp	olive oil
2 cloves	garlic, minced
1	large red onion, chopped
3 cups	calamari rings
4	medium tomatoes, chopped
1/2 cup	dry red wine
1/2 cup	orange juice
1/2 cup	water
1/4 cup	chopped fresh coriander
1/4 cup	freshly squeezed lemon juice
1 tbsp	lemon rind
1 tsp	brown sugar
1/2 tsp	tomato paste
	Lemon wedges, for garnish

In a large sauté pan or skillet heat the oil; sauté the garlic and onion until onion is translucent, about 2 minutes. Add the calamari and sauté 3–4 minutes, until it turns white. Add the tomatoes, red wine, orange juice, water, coriander, lemon juice, lemon rind, brown sugar and tomato paste. Reduce heat to medium and simmer 8–10 minutes, until calamari is tender. Garnish with lemon wedges. Serve with French bread for dipping.

VARIATIONS:

- REPLACE CALAMARI WITH JUMBO SHRIMP OR SCALLOPS.
- REPLACE CALAMARI WITH ASSORTED FRESHLY CHOPPED VEGETABLES.

Low-Fat Options:

- REPLACE RED WINE WITH GRAPE JUICE.
- SAUTÉ IN 1/4 CUP OF VEGETABLE STOCK RATHER THAN OIL.

Health Option:

- REPLACE BROWN SUGAR WITH CALORIE-REDUCED LIQUID SWEETENER.

Sautéed Crabmeat Bruschetta
SERVES 4–6

Wine adds a richness to any dish, and simmering for several minutes ensures that its mellow flavor is imparted into the food—in this case, crabmeat. This recipe is a slight departure from everyday bruschetta, and I devised it especially for the crabmeat lover. I prefer this appetizer to have a real bite, but I have made it considerably milder for some of my guests.

2 tbsp	butter
2 cloves	garlic, minced
1/4 cup	finely chopped celery
1/2	sweet red pepper, chopped
1/2 lb	fresh crabmeat
1/2 cup	chopped green onions
1/2 cup	chopped fresh parsley
1/4 cup	dry white wine
2 tbsp	lemon juice
1/2 tsp	crushed red pepper flakes
1/2 tsp	paprika
1/2 tsp	salt
1/2 tsp	black pepper
1	medium tomato, chopped
1 tbsp	balsamic vinegar
6 slices	toasted French bread

VARIATIONS:

- FOR A VEGETARIAN VERSION, REPLACE CRABMEAT WITH 2 CUPS OF CHOPPED MUSHROOMS.
- REPLACE CRABMEAT WITH SHRIMP.

Low-Fat Option:

- REPLACE BUTTER WITH A VEGETABLE COOKING SPRAY.

In a large sauté pan or skillet melt the butter; sauté the garlic, celery, and sweet red pepper until softened, about 2 minutes. Stir in the crabmeat, green onions, parsley, white wine, lemon juice, red pepper flakes, paprika, salt and pepper; simmer another 3 minutes. Add the tomato. Mix well and stir in the balsamic vinegar. Serve warm on toasted French bread.

Stuffed Crab
SERVES 2-4

I have been told that there are more than 4,500 varieties of crab. When you're shopping you'll probably find the more common Dungeness or blue crab, which is no more than eight inches across. Its delicious combination of dark and white "meat" creates this scrumptious dish, courtesy of the Mini Club on St. Martin in the Caribbean, where the chef hand-picked the crab for my lunch. It was a treat I haven't had repeated. You can avoid the work of preparing live crabs and just buy cooked crabmeat at the supermarket.

1/3	baguette
8	crabs
1	onion, chopped
12	chives
4	large carrots, chopped
1 cup	chopped fresh parsley
1 tsp	dried thyme
	Salt and black pepper to taste
1	green chile, chopped
1 tbsp	butter, softened
	Juice of 1 lime

While preparing the crabs, soak the baguette, broken into small pieces, in water. (Squeeze water out before using.) Carefully scrub and wash the crabs. Cook the crabs in a large pot of boiling water with the onion, 2 chives, carrot, parsley and thyme for 15 minutes. Add the salt and pepper; set aside to cool. Meanwhile, chop remaining chives.

Shell the crabs, reserving the shells and discarding innards. In a saucepan combine the remaining chives, green chile, butter and lime juice. Add the crabmeat and bread; stir well and leave to cook, uncovered, on medium heat for 10 minutes, gently stirring occasionally. Fill the shells with crabmeat mixture and serve immediately.

⊙ *Recipe from the Mini Club, St. Martin.*

VARIATION:

⊙ REPLACE CRABMEAT WITH I LB CHOPPED SHRIMP.

Health Option:

⊙ USE A CALORIE-REDUCED BUTTER OR MARGARINE.

Shrimp Sautéed with Garlic and Mango

SERVES 4

Garlic has such a rich history. In its raw state it is believed to have magical healing powers and, of course, it was worn to ward off evil spirits and vampires. My own interest in garlic is simple—taste! It adds its delicate flavor to this shrimp appetizer, which can be tossed with any pasta for a main dish.

2 tbsp	olive oil
1 tsp	sesame oil
4 cloves	garlic, minced
1/2 cup	chopped sweet red pepper
12	jumbo shrimp, peeled
1 cup	chopped mango
1/2 cup	chopped green onions
1/2 cup	finely chopped fresh parsley
1/2 tsp	sesame seeds
1/2 tsp	crushed red pepper flakes
1/2 tsp	salt
1/2 tsp	black pepper
2	mandarin oranges, for garnish

In a large sauté pan or skillet heat the olive oil and sesame oil; sauté the garlic and sweet red pepper for 1 minute. Add the shrimp and sauté another 2 minutes. Stir in mango, green onions, parsley, sesame seeds, red pepper flakes, salt and pepper; reduce heat and cook another minute. Serve on top of a small mixed salad. Garnish with mandarin orange sections.

VARIATIONS:

- REPLACE THE SHRIMP WITH 16 LARGE SCALLOPS.
- REPLACE THE MANGO WITH AN EQUAL AMOUNT OF PAPAYA OR ORANGE.

Low-Fat Option:

- SAUTÉ WITH ABOUT 1/4 CUP OF VEGETABLE STOCK INSTEAD OF OLIVE OIL.

Ken's Orange Shrimp Cocktail

SERVES 4

Shrimp cocktail is one of my favorite appetizers. I like the idea that it can be prepared in advance and chilled in the refrigerator. Michel Roux, master chef of the Century cruise ship, does a couple of types but this is my quick version.

8	asparagus spears
2 cups	mixed salad greens
16	large jumbo or tiger shrimp, cleaned, peeled (tails still on) and cooked
2	oranges, cut into 16 slices
2 tbsp	balsamic vinegar
1 tsp	lemon juice
1 tbsp	orange juice, with pulp
1/2 tsp	brown sugar
1 tbsp	orange rind
2 tbsp	finely chopped chives, for garnish
	Black pepper to taste

In a deep sauté pan or skillet blanch asparagus by placing it in boiling water for 2 minutes. Remove and place in very cold water or ice water to retain crispness and color. Meanwhile, evenly divide the salad greens onto four salad plates. Alternate one shrimp, then one orange slice, using four each per plate, in a circle on top of the salad. In a small mixing bowl combine the balsamic vinegar, lemon juice, orange juice and brown sugar; mix with a fork. Place 2 asparagus spears in an X on top of the shrimp and orange. Using a teaspoon sprinkle the sauce on each salad and garnish with the orange rind and chives.

VARIATIONS:

⊚ REPLACE THE SHRIMP WITH 2 LOBSTER TAILS, SLICED.

⊚ FOR A VEGETARIAN VERSION, REPLACE SHRIMP WITH 2 LARGE PORTOBELLO MUSHROOMS, GRILLED AND SLICED.

Health Option:

⊚ REPLACE BROWN SUGAR WITH A CALORIE-REDUCED LIQUID SWEETENER.

Smoked Salmon Stuffed with Curried Cream Cheese and Asparagus

SERVES 4–6

The term "curry powder" was coined in India by British colonials. Curry (used often in Caribbean cooking because of the many East Indians who settled there in the nineteenth century) is a blend of spices indigenous to India that are known as masalas, and that range from mild to very hot. This appetizer recipe calls for mild curry powder—the perfect complement.

3/4 cup	cream cheese, softened
1/2	sweet red pepper, finely chopped
2 cloves	garlic, minced
1/4 cup	chopped fresh dill
1/2 tsp	mild curry powder
1/4 tsp	crushed red pepper flakes
1/4 tsp	black pepper
6 slices	smoked salmon
6	asparagus spears
	Juice of 1 lemon

In a mixing bowl combine the cream cheese, sweet red pepper, garlic, dill, curry powder, red pepper flakes and pepper. Arrange salmon slices skin side down and spread with cream cheese mixture. Meanwhile, grill or broil the asparagus, coating with the lemon juice before and during grilling. Place an asparagus spear on a diagonal at one end of a salmon slice and roll up to surround asparagus. Repeat with remaining asparagus.

VARIATIONS:

- REPLACE ASPARAGUS WITH GRILLED SHRIMP.
- REPLACE SMOKED SALMON WITH GRILLED EGGPLANT.
- REPLACE CURRY POWDER WITH CHILI POWDER

Low-Fat Option:

- USE LOW-FAT CREAM CHEESE.

Hot and Spicy Salmon Fishcakes with Island Fruit

SERVES 4–6

If you lived on one of the beautiful Caribbean islands you might stroll out your kitchen door, reach high into a tree with a pole and pull down a ripe papaya fruit. Here at home you'll have to content yourself with the local market or a grocery store where you trust the produce is fresh. Wherever you buy it, papaya makes a fabulous contribution to these hot and spicy fishcakes. This appetizer will doubtless whet the appetite for other culinary island treasures to come!

3	salmon steaks
1 cup	orange juice
2 cloves	garlic, minced
1	egg, lightly beaten
1	small apple or pear, chopped
1/2 cup	dry bread crumbs
1/2 cup	chopped green onions
1/2 cup	chopped papaya
1/2 cup	chopped mango
1/4 cup	chopped fresh coriander
1/2 tsp	paprika
1/2 tsp	crushed red pepper flakes
1/2 tsp	brown sugar
1/2 tsp	salt
1/2 tsp	black pepper

In a large skillet over medium heat, poach the salmon steaks in the orange juice 4–5 minutes or until light pink, turning once. Remove salmon and let cool. Discard the skin and bones. Crumble salmon into a medium bowl and combine well with remaining ingredients. If mixture is dry, add 1 tbsp of vegetable oil. Shape into six patties and broil for 10 minutes, turning once. (You can also pan fry the fishcakes in a little oil or in a nonstick pan with vegetable cooking spray.)

VARIATION:

⊚ REPLACE SALMON STEAKS WITH ANY FIRM FISH OR WITH 3/4 CUP OF CRABMEAT.

Low-Fat Option:

⊚ REPLACE SALMON STEAKS WITH A 1-LB BLOCK OF CALORIE-REDUCED FIRM TOFU. IF IT'S TOO DRY ADD 2 TBSP OF NON-FAT YOGURT.

Health Option:

⊚ USE A CALORIE-REDUCED LIQUID SWEETENER OR LEAVE OUT THE SUGAR.

Soups

Chilled Banana-Pineapple-Coconut Soup

SERVES 4

Chilled soup is one of the most nutritious foods we can eat—the freshest of ingredients being puréed together, immediately capturing all of the vitamins and minerals. Fittingly, soups have fairly recently acquired a definite glamor, their preparation and consumption becoming an adventure. You'll see what I mean when you taste this very Caribbean example.

4	bananas
1 cup	chopped pineapple
3 cups	pineapple juice
1 cup	plain yogurt
1 cup	apple juice
1/2 cup	unsweetened coconut milk
1/4 cup	unsweetened coconut flakes
1/2 tsp	cinnamon
1/4 tsp	ground nutmeg

Combine all ingredients in a food processor; blend well. (You may have to work in batches.) Chill the soup at least 1 hour before serving. Garnish with a sprinkle of cinnamon.

VARIATION:

- REPLACE THE PINEAPPLE WITH OTHER FRUIT. TRY STRAWBERRIES.

Low-Fat Option:

- USE LOW-FAT OR NON-FAT YOGURT.

Chilled Peach Soup with Mint

SERVES 4

This cold soup is quick and efficient to prepare. I have made it on various occasions and my guests have all loved it.

6	medium peaches, chopped
2 cups	orange juice
2 cups	peach nectar
2 cups	plain yogurt
2 tbsp	chopped fresh parsley
2 tbsp	chopped fresh mint
1 tbsp	lemon juice
1 tsp	brown sugar

In a food processor combine all ingredients; purée until smooth. You may have to do two batches or use a large bowl and a hand blender. Chill well before serving.

VARIATIONS:

⊙ REPLACE THE PEACHES WITH PEARS AND USE PEAR NECTAR.

⊙ TO MAKE A COLD MANDARIN SOUP, REPLACE THE PEACHES WITH MANDARIN ORANGES AND USE ONLY ORANGE JUICE.

Low-Fat Option:

⊙ USE NON-FAT OR LOW-FAT YOGURT.

Health Option:

⊙ REPLACE BROWN SUGAR WITH A CALORIE-REDUCED LIQUID SWEETENER.

Chilled Apple Soup
SERVES 4

The apple, of the Rosaceae family, has been around for at least 6,500 years. Considered the king of fruits, the apple has played a part in religion, magic, superstition, folklore, history and medicine as far back as we can go. Take a chance and serve this soup all year round. The nice thing about chilled soups is that they clear the palate.

4	apples, peeled and chopped
2 cups	apple juice
1/2	lemon
1/8	cinnamon stick
1/2 cup	sour cream
1 tbsp	lemon juice

In a soup pot bring to a boil the apples, apple juice, lemon and cinnamon stick; boil for 5 minutes. Discard the cinnamon stick. Purée in a blender or with a hand blender. Cool in the refrigerator. Whisk in the sour cream and lemon juice. Chill well before serving.

VARIATION:

⊙ REPLACE THE APPLE JUICE WITH PEAR JUICE AND THE APPLE WITH PEARS. (I HAVE MADE THIS VERSION SEVERAL TIMES AND EACH TIME MY GUESTS WANT SECONDS.)

⊙ ADD A SUGAR OR A CALORIE-REDUCED SWEETER.

Low-Fat Option:

⊙ REPLACE THE SOUR CREAM WITH 1 CUP OF NON-FAT YOGURT (MIX WELL) OR USE NON-FAT SOUR CREAM.

Chilled Pear and Apple Soup with Coconut

SERVES 6

Nothing is more flavorful than the combination of pears and apples, mixed with a hint of cinnamon from the islands.

3	pears, cored and peeled
3	apples, cored and peeled
2 cups	pear nectar
2 cups	apple juice
1/2 cup	dry white wine
2 tbsp	apple juice concentrate
1/2 tsp	cinnamon
1/4 tsp	ground nutmeg
1 cup	whipping cream
2 tbsp	unsweetened coconut

In a large mixing bowl combine the pears, apples, pear nectar, apple juice, wine, apple juice concentrate, cinnamon and nutmeg. In a food processor purée mixture (in batches, if necessary). Once the entire mixture is blended, mix in the whipping cream and garnish with a little coconut on top before serving.

VARIATION:

⊚ SUBSTITUTE PEACHES AND PEACH JUICE FOR APPLES AND JUICE .

Low-Fat Option:

⊚ REPLACE CREAM WITH EITHER LOW-FAT OR NON-FAT YOGURT.

Health Option:

⊚ REPLACE THE APPLE JUICE CONCENTRATE WITH A LIQUID SWEETENER.

⊚ *Recipe from Estate St. Peter Greathouse, St. Thomas, U.S. Virgin Islands.*

Chilled Strawberry Soup
SERVES 6

Strawberry soup can be enjoyed all year long and it serves as a good introduction to a heavier meal that might contain meats or heavy sauces.

1 pkg	frozen unsweetened strawberries
2 cups	cranberry juice
1/2 cup	dry red wine
2 tbsp	brown sugar
1/4 tsp	cinnamon
2 cups	strawberry yogurt
1/2 cup	cream
2 tbsp	chopped fresh mint
1/2 cup	sliced fresh strawberries for garnish

In a large mixing bowl combine the strawberries, cranberry juice, wine, brown sugar, cinnamon, yogurt, cream and mint. Transfer to food processor (in batches, if necessary) and purée. Chill about 1 hour prior to serving. Serve in individual bowls with sliced fresh strawberries as garnish.

VARIATION:

⊙ REPLACE THE FROZEN STRAWBERRIES WITH FROZEN CRANBERRIES, THEN ADD FRESH CRANBERRIES FOR THE GARNISH OF THE SOUP.

Low-Fat Options:

⊙ REPLACE THE YOGURT WITH A NON-FAT YOGURT.

⊙ REPLACE CREAM WITH SKIM MILK.

Health Option:

⊙ REPLACE BROWN SUGAR WITH A CALORIE-REDUCED LIQUID SWEETENER.

Avocado and Salsa Soup

SERVES 6

A lot of viewers ask me for recipes that include avocado. The avocado gives any recipe a rich, smooth taste. Try this soup and tell me what you think.

1 tbsp	vegetable oil
1	medium red onion, chopped
2 cloves	garlic, minced
1	sweet green pepper, chopped
4	avocados, diced
1 can	stewed tomatoes, diced (19 oz/540 mL)
5 cups	vegetable stock
1/2 cup	chopped fresh parsley
1/4 cup	chopped fresh coriander
1/4 cup	chopped fresh mint
1/4 cup	chopped fresh basil
1	jalapeño pepper, chopped
1	bay leaf
1 tbsp	lemon juice
1/2 tsp	salt
1/2 tsp	black pepper
2 tbsp	chopped chives, for garnish

In a deep soup pot heat the oil; sauté the onion and garlic for 2 minutes. Add the green pepper and sauté another 2 minutes. Add avocados, tomatoes, vegetable stock, parsley, coriander, mint, basil, jalapeño pepper, bay leaf, lemon juice, salt and pepper; simmer, uncovered and stirring occasionally, 20 minutes. Discard the bay leaf. Purée the soup with a hand blender or in a food processor. Serve garnished with chopped chives.

VARIATIONS:

⊚ REPLACE STEWED TOMATOES WITH 4 LARGE PLUM TOMATOES, CHOPPED, 1 CUP WATER AND 1 TSP OF TOMATO PASTE.

⊚ REPLACE THE VEGETABLE STOCK WITH CHICKEN STOCK.

⊚ ADD 1 CUP OF TABLE CREAM IF DESIRED.

Low-Fat Option:

⊚ REPLACE THE AVOCADO WITH 4 MEDIUM TOMATOES, CHOPPED.

Sopa de Frijoles

SERVES 8

No Mexican meal is complete without beans. Black beans, small, shiny and kidney-shaped, have a slightly sweet flavor and are the essential ingredient of the majestic Brazilian **feijoada**, a rich stew. This Mexican black bean soup from Panchos Backyard in Cozumel sometimes has a special touch—ground toasted laurel leaves (bay leaves).

4 cups	cooked black beans
3 tbsp	olive oil
2 cloves	garlic, finely chopped
1	jalapeño pepper, seeded and finely chopped
1/2	white onion, finely chopped
1/4 tsp	ground bay leaves
1/4 tsp	ground oregano
1/4 tsp	cumin
4 cups	beef consommé or beef stock
2 tbsp	dry sherry
	Salt and black pepper

Low-Fat Option:

◎ REPLACE THE OLIVE OIL WITH A VEGETABLE OIL LOWER IN SATURATED FATS OR CALORIE REDUCED.

Health Option:

◎ USE A LOW-SODIUM BEEF CONSOMMÉ OR BEEF STOCK.

Mash the black beans slightly, just enough to break the beans into smaller pieces; set aside. In a large saucepan over medium heat, heat the olive oil; add the garlic, jalapeño pepper, onion, bay leaves, oregano and cumin. Cook, stirring, until the onion is slightly golden. Stir in the consommé and the black beans. Increase the heat to medium-high and bring soup to a boil, stirring frequently to prevent beans from sticking to the bottom of the pot. As the soup begins to boil, slowly stir in the sherry. Add salt and pepper to taste, stir well and remove from heat. Serve with garlic bread and a side plate of diced tomatoes and onions.

◎ *Recipe from Pancho's Backyard Restaurant, Cozumel, Mexico.*

Mexican Black Bean Soup with Salsa and Corn

SERVES 4–6

This black bean soup can be a meal in itself. My version is a little lower in calories but still very flavorful.

1 tbsp	olive oil
1	medium red onion, chopped
2 cloves	garlic, minced
5 cups	vegetable stock
1 cup	mild or hot salsa
1/4 cup	chopped fresh dill
1/4 cup	chopped fresh basil
1 tsp	chili powder
1/2 tsp	salt
1/2 tsp	black pepper
1	bay leaf
1 cup	cooked black beans
1/2 cup	cooked corn
2 tbsp	low-fat sour cream, for garnish
1/2 cup	chopped chives, for garnish

VARIATION:

⊚ SUBSTITUTE RED OR WHITE BEANS FOR THE BLACK BEANS.

Low-Fat Option:

⊚ USE 2 TBSP OF VEGETABLE STOCK INSTEAD OF OLIVE OIL FOR SAUTÉING.

In a large soup pot or slow cooker heat the olive oil; sauté the onion for 1 minute. Add the garlic and sauté for another 2 minutes or until onion is translucent; be careful not to burn the garlic. Add stock, salsa, dill, basil, chili powder, salt, pepper and bay leaf. Bring to a boil, reduce heat and simmer, uncovered and stirring occasionally, 20 minutes. Stir in the black beans and corn; cook another 2 minutes. Discard bay leaf. Serve in bowls garnished with a dollop of sour cream and chives.

Carrot and Ginger Soup
SERVES 4-6

Mixing carrot with ginger is an island favorite. Not only is this soup delicious but it is also colorful, which makes a wonderful presentation. Here's one of my secrets: occasionally I buy ground-up carrot baby food and add that to the soup. It truly makes the soup richer in texture.

1 tbsp	vegetable oil
1	medium onion, chopped
2 cloves	garlic, minced
1	sweet red pepper, chopped
4 cups	chopped carrots
6 cups	vegetable stock
1 cup	apple juice
1/4 cup	chopped fresh basil
1/4 cup	chopped fresh dill
2 tbsp	chopped fresh ginger
1 tsp	chopped fresh thyme
1/2 tsp	paprika
1/2 tsp	salt
1/2 tsp	black pepper
1	bay leaf
1/2 cup	table cream (optional)

Heat the vegetable oil in a large soup pot; sauté the onion and garlic for 2 minutes. Add the red pepper and sauté another 2 minutes. Add carrots, stock, apple juice, basil, dill, ginger, thyme, paprika, salt, pepper and bay leaf; bring to a boil. Reduce the heat to medium and simmer, uncovered and stirring occasionally, 20 minutes. Discard the bay leaf. Purée the soup until smooth using a hand blender or food processor. For a creamier consistency, fold in table cream at the very end.

Sweet Red Pepper Soup

SERVES 4-6

The Sweet Red Pepper Soup is exactly the way it sounds. It has a mild, gentle flavor that will get you lots of compliments when you serve it.

2 tbsp	olive oil
1	medium onion, chopped
6	sweet red peppers, chopped
5 cups	vegetable stock
4	plum tomatoes, chopped
1	bay leaf
2 tbsp	chopped fresh basil
1 tbsp	chopped fresh mint
1 tsp	brown sugar
1/2 tsp	paprika
1/2 tsp	salt
1/2 tsp	black pepper
1 cup	table cream

In a large soup pot heat the olive oil; sauté the onion for 1 minute. Add the red peppers and sauté another 3 minutes, stirring well. Add the vegetable stock, tomatoes, bay leaf, basil, mint, brown sugar, paprika, salt and pepper. Bring to a boil, reduce heat and simmer 20 minutes, stirring occasionally. Discard bay leaf. With a hand blender or in a food processor blend the soup until a creamy consistency. Return to the pot, slowly fold in the cream, heat through and serve.

VARIATION:

⊙ REPLACE THE SWEET RED PEPPERS WITH 5 CUPS CHOPPED MUSHROOMS TO CREATE A WONDERFUL MUSHROOM SOUP.

Low-Fat Option:

⊙ LEAVE OUT THE TABLE CREAM AND ADD 1 MORE CUP OF VEGETABLE STOCK. FOR A CREAMIER TEXTURE, ADD 2 POTATOES COOKED IN VEGETABLE STOCK. PURÉE WITH THE OTHER INGREDIENTS.

Butternut Squash Soup with Cinnamon
SERVES 4–6

This soup is an island favorite. Occasionally a *touch* of curry is added.

6 cups	vegetable stock
3 cups	chopped butternut squash
1	medium onion, chopped
1	large potato, cubed
1	bay leaf
1 tsp	brown sugar
1/2 tsp	dried basil
1/2 tsp	dried oregano
1/2 tsp	cinnamon
1/2 tsp	salt
1/2 tsp	black pepper
1/4 tsp	ground cloves
1/4 tsp	ground nutmeg
1 cup	table cream

In a large soup pot bring the stock to a boil. Add squash, onion, potato, bay leaf, brown sugar, basil, oregano, cinnamon, salt, pepper, cloves and nutmeg. Boil the soup until the squash and potato are tender, about 30 minutes. Discard the bay leaf. Purée the soup with a hand blender or in a food processor. Gently fold in the cream.

VARIATIONS:

- REPLACE THE VEGETABLE STOCK WITH CHICKEN STOCK.
- REPLACE THE BUTTERNUT SQUASH WITH PUMPKIN.

Low-Fat Option:

- REPLACE THE TABLE CREAM WITH LOW-FAT SOY MILK OR NON-FAT MILK BEVERAGE.

Health Option:

- REPLACE THE BROWN SUGAR WITH CALORIE-REDUCED LIQUID SWEETENER.

Hot and Sour Soup

SERVES 4–6

The combination of hot and sour was initially an oriental recipe, and this version is prepared several different ways in the Caribbean.

5 cups	chicken or beef stock
4 cloves	garlic, crushed
2	carrots, julienned
1 cup	chopped mushrooms
1 cup	table cream
1/2 cup	apple juice
1/4 cup	light soy sauce
2 tbsp	dry sherry (optional)
2 tbsp	rice wine vinegar
1 tbsp	lemon juice
1 tsp	chopped fresh ginger
1 tsp	brown sugar
1 tsp	balsamic vinegar
1/2 tsp	dried basil
1 cup	cubed tofu
1/4 cup	chopped chives, for garnish

In a large soup pot bring the stock to a boil. Add garlic, carrots, mushrooms, cream, apple juice, soy sauce, sherry (if using), wine vinegar, lemon juice, ginger, brown sugar, balsamic vinegar and basil. Reduce heat and simmer, uncovered and stirring occasionally, for 15 minutes or until vegetables are tender. Stir in the tofu and bring to a boil. Taste; if the soup requires a bit more sugar, add another 1/2 tsp. Serve soup sprinkled with fresh chives.

VARIATION:

○ REPLACE THE TOFU WITH CUBED CHICKEN.

Health Options:

○ REPLACE BROWN SUGAR WITH A CALORIE-REDUCED LIQUID SWEETENER.

○ USE A LOW-SODIUM VEGETABLE STOCK.

Pepperpot with Chèvre
SERVES 4

The Caribbean islands have several versions of pepperpot soup.
The common thread is the inclusion of various types of peppers,
which determine whether the soup is mild, hot, very hot or fiery! My
version with chèvre, or goat cheese, is on the medium side of hot, but
the enchanting flavor is what makes this soup delectable.

2 lb	cubed lean beef
1 tbsp	vegetable oil
2 cloves	garlic, finely chopped
1	large onion, chopped
3	sweet red peppers, chopped
1 cup	cubed squash
2	hot peppers, chopped
1 tsp	chopped fresh thyme
1 tsp	cayenne
1/4 tsp	cinnamon
	Salt and black pepper to taste
4 cups	vegetable stock
1/2 cup	crumbled mild goat cheese
2 tsp	chopped fresh coriander

In a large soup pot brown the beef in vegetable oil.
Remove beef and add the garlic and onion and sauté
for 2 minutes. Add the sweet peppers and squash;
sauté for 2 minutes. Add the hot peppers, thyme,
cayenne, cinnamon, salt, pepper and vegetable stock.
Return beef to pot. Bring to a boil, reduce heat and
simmer for 15–20 minutes or until vegetables are
tender. About 5 minutes before serving, stir in the goat
cheese and coriander.

VARIATION:

⊚ REPLACE THE GOAT
  CHEESE WITH BLUE
  CHEESE OR STILTON.

Low-Fat Option:

⊚ REPLACE BEEF WITH
  CUBED TURKEY.

Health Option:

⊚ USE LOW-SODIUM BEEF
  STOCK.

Curry Soup with Pork and Apple

SERVES 4–6

The combination of lean pork and apple really works well. In this recipe you can use leftover pork roast or pork chops that have all of the fat removed.

1 tbsp	vegetable oil
1	medium onion, chopped
2 cloves	garlic, minced
1	apple, chopped
5 cups	chicken stock
1 cup	apple juice (approx.)
1/2 cup	frozen peas
1 tsp	mild curry powder
1/2 tsp	black pepper
1/2 tsp	dried basil
1/4 tsp	salt
1/4 tsp	cinnamon
1/4 tsp	ground nutmeg
1	bay leaf
1 cup	cubed cooked pork
1/2 cup	cooked rice
1/2 cup	chopped green onions, for garnish

In a deep soup pot heat the oil; sauté the onion and garlic for 2 minutes. Stir in apple, chicken stock, apple juice, peas, curry powder, pepper, basil, salt, cinnamon, nutmeg and bay leaf. Bring to a boil, reduce heat and simmer, uncovered and stirring occasionally, 20 minutes. If liquid reduces too much, add more apple juice. Stir in the pork and rice; simmer another 5 minutes or until pork is heated through. Discard bay leaf. Serve garnished with chopped green onion.

VARIATIONS:

◎ REPLACE APPLE AND APPLE JUICE WITH PEAR AND PEAR JUICE.

◎ FOR A RICHER SOUP, ADD 1/2 CUP OF APPLE-SAUCE.

Low-Fat Option:

◎ REPLACE THE PORK WITH TURKEY BREAST.

Conch Chowder

SERVES 4

Secluded on two acres next to Love Beach is Compass Point, a
surprising arrangement of vibrantly colored huts on stilts. My stay
here in Nassau, in the Bahamas, was surpassed only by the excellent
dishes I sampled at the Compass Point Restaurant, further enhanced
by the oceanfront view. I began one meal with this Conch Chowder,
made with one of my favorite seafoods, and it tantalized my taste
buds for delights yet to come. You can find conch at some
supermarkets, as well as at fish markets.

1/4 cup	canola oil or vegetable oil
4	skinless conch, finely chopped
1 tbsp	dried thyme OR 1 sprig fresh thyme
1/4	scotch bonnet pepper, finely chopped
1 tsp	crushed black pepper
3	bay leaves
1	large onion, coarsely chopped
1	celery stalk, coarsely chopped
1	sweet red pepper, coarsely chopped
1	large potato, coarsely chopped
1	large carrot, coarsely chopped
1/2 cup	flour
2 tbsp	butter
8 cups	fish stock or water
	Salt to taste

VARIATION:

⊙ REPLACE THE CONCH
WITH AN ASSORTMENT
OF SEAFOOD: TRY
CLAMS, SHRIMP,
SCALLOPS OR
SWORDFISH.

Low-Fat Option:

⊙ REPLACE THE BUTTER
WITH A LOW-FAT
BUTTER OR MARGARINE.

In a deep soup pot heat the oil; add the conch, thyme,
chile pepper, crushed black pepper and bay leaves.
Cook for 5–7 minutes, stirring often. Add the onion,
celery, red pepper, potato, carrot, flour and butter; cook
for another 5 minutes. Add the fish stock, bring to a
boil, reduce heat and simmer for 10 minutes. Add salt
to taste.

⊙ *Recipe from Compass Point Beach Club, Nassau, Bahamas.*

Gazpacho Frio Con Langosta

SERVES 4

The traditional gazpacho, Spanish in origin, is a simple cold soup of cucumber, tomato, sweet pepper and moistened bread. This version with Mexican overtones was a real treat the afternoon I visited Cozumel. It takes no time to prepare and is a perfect do-ahead recipe for a dinner party.

I	4-oz lobster tail
2 slices	white bread, crusts removed
1/2 cup	chilled water
7	parsley stems
3	plum tomatoes, chopped
I	sweet green pepper, diced
I	celery stalk, chopped
I clove	garlic, chopped
1/4	white onion, chopped
I cup	tomato juice
I tbsp	virgin olive oil
1/4 tsp	salt
Pinch	black pepper
1/4	seedless cucumber, peeled and chopped

Boil the lobster tail in 1 cup of salted water for 10 minutes; drain, chill and set aside for garnish. Cut the bread into eight rounds and toast for croutons; set aside. In a blender or food processor blend the water, parsley, tomatoes, half the green pepper, celery, garlic, onion, tomato juice, olive oil, salt and pepper until smooth. Strain mixture over a bowl and discard solids. Chill the gazpacho. Sprinkle diced lobster and remaining green pepper on top of the gazpacho. Serve with cucumber and croutons on the side.

VARIATION:

- REPLACE THE LOBSTER TAIL WITH 4–6 PEELED JUMBO SHRIMP, BOILED AND DICED.

Low-Fat Options:

- REPLACE THE WHITE BREAD WITH WHOLE-WHEAT BREAD.
- REPLACE THE VIRGIN OLIVE OIL WITH A VEGETABLE OIL LOWER IN SATURATED FATS OR A CALORIE-REDUCED OIL.

◎ *Recipe from Pancho's Backyard Restaurant, Cozumel, Mexico.*

Shrimp and Curry Soup
SERVES 4

When I have a dinner party I usually serve a small bowl of soup at the beginning of the meal. Here is one favorite with my guests.

4 cups	chicken stock
2 cloves	garlic, minced
1/2 cup	chopped fresh coriander
1/4 cup	chopped fresh basil
1 tbsp	lemon juice
1 tsp	mild curry powder
1/2 tsp	salt
1/2 tsp	black pepper
1/2 tsp	Dijon mustard
1	bay leaf
1-1/2 cups	shrimp, peeled
1 cup	table cream
1/4 cup	chopped fresh parsley, for garnish

In a soup pot bring the chicken stock to a boil. Stir in the garlic, coriander, basil, lemon juice, curry powder, salt, pepper, mustard and bay leaf. Simmer 15 minutes. Gently stir in the shrimp and cream. Simmer until shrimp are cooked through; do not boil. Discard bay leaf. Serve garnished with parsley.

VARIATION:

◎ REPLACE THE SHRIMP WITH 1-1/2 CUPS OF CUBED COOKED CHICKEN AND ADD COOKED RICE IF DESIRED.

Low-Fat Options:

◎ REPLACE CHICKEN STOCK WITH VEGETABLE STOCK.

◎ REPLACE TABLE CREAM WITH NON-FAT MILK.

Spicy Caribbean Seafood Soup with Pasta

SERVES 4–6

I often serve this soup as a main course. You can use your favorite seafood or whatever is in season.

2 tbsp	olive oil
1	medium red onion, chopped
4 cloves	garlic, minced
4	celery stalks, chopped
2	carrots, chopped
1	sweet green pepper, chopped
1 can	stewed tomatoes, diced (19 oz/540 mL)
6 cups	fish stock or vegetable stock
1/2 tsp	dried basil
1/2 tsp	dried oregano
1/2 tsp	cayenne
1/2 tsp	salt
1/2 tsp	black pepper
1 cup	canned clams
1/2 cup	small scallops
1/2 cup	elbow pasta

In a deep soup pot heat the oil; sauté the onion and garlic for 3 minutes, being careful not to burn the garlic. Add the celery, carrots and green pepper; gently sauté another 3 minutes. Add tomatoes, fish stock, basil, oregano, cayenne, salt and pepper. Bring to a boil, reduce heat and simmer 15 minutes, stirring occasionally. Stir in clams, scallops and pasta. Simmer until pasta is cooked, 5–7 minutes.

VARIATIONS:

⊙ REPLACE THE SEAFOOD WITH CUBED SWORDFISH OR TUNA OR A WHITE FISH LIKE SOLE. KEEP IN MIND THAT IT WILL START TO FLAKE.

Low-Fat Option:

⊙ SAUTÉ IN SOUP STOCK INSTEAD OF OIL.

Salads

Mezclun with Chèvre and Mango Vinaigrette

SERVES 4

Mezclun is a potpourri of lettuces, chicories, cresses, arugula and chervil. Arugula is an old-fashioned salad herb that looks like radish or young turnip tops. It's enjoying a great revival in Britain and North America. Traditional mezclun mixes are strong; the Italians, for example, lace it with the bitter radicchio lettuce. Chèvre, of course, is the French word for goat cheese. It comes in a variety of flavors and is often named after its place of origin.

1	large mango, chopped
6 oz	chèvre, softened
1	shallot, minced
1	egg yolk
3/4 cup	olive oil
1/4 cup	white wine vinegar
	Salt and black pepper
2 cups	mezclun (mixed greens)

Purée mango in a blender. In a bowl whisk together mango purée, chèvre, shallot and egg yolk. Slowly whisk in the oil alternating with the vinegar. Season to taste. Arrange mezclun on salad plates and drizzle with vinaigrette.

Ken grilling deck-side on board the Century.
(top right) By the staircase of the Century's grand dining room. *Jamie Hanson*

Low-Fat Caribbean Coleslaw

SERVES 4

This salad can be turned into a main course by adding cooked chicken, seafood or, to keep it vegetarian, tofu. The bonus is that the coleslaw is very low in fat.

4 cups	shredded cabbage
4	carrots, shredded
3	oranges, quartered and seeded
I	sweet red pepper, cut into strips
I	sweet green pepper, cut into strips
I	medium red onion, sliced in rings
1/4 cup	chopped fresh coriander
1/4 cup	chopped fresh parsley
I tbsp	orange rind
2 tbsp	slivered almonds, for garnish

DRESSING

1/4 cup	orange juice, pulp included
I tbsp	light soy sauce
I tbsp	balsamic vinegar
I tbsp	rice wine vinegar
I tbsp	lemon juice
I tbsp	orange rind
1/4 tsp	cayenne

In a large mixing bowl combine cabbage, carrots, oranges, red pepper, green pepper, onion, coriander, parsley and orange rind. Combine all the dressing ingredients in a jar and shake until well mixed. Pour the dressing over the salad and toss well. Sprinkle with slivered almonds.

VARIATION:

◎ REPLACE THE FRESH CORIANDER WITH MORE FRESH PARSLEY; IT CHANGES THE TASTE SLIGHTLY.

Carrot and Ginger Soup (page 42), Sesame Tofu Cubes (page 20) and Low-Fat Caribbean Coleslaw (opposite). *Linda Corbett, food styled by Johanna Weinstein*

Ken's Favorite Fruit Salad

SERVES 4

This fruit salad can be served as a starter or a main course, and also as a dessert. You decide! The placement of the fruit is very important to the presentation of this dish. Be sure to use the lemon juice to prevent discoloring of the bananas, pears and apples.

4	mandarin oranges, peeled and quartered
2	bananas, halved and sliced lengthwise
2	mangoes, cut into wide strips
2	kiwifruit, peeled and sliced
2	pears, cored and sliced
2	apples, sliced
1/2	honeydew melon, seeded and sliced lengthwise
1 cup	halved strawberries
1 tsp	lemon juice
2 cups	watercress

DRESSING

3/4 cup	fruit yogurt
1/2 cup	sliced strawberries
1/2 cup	orange juice
1 tsp	chopped fresh mint
1 tsp	liquid honey

VARIATION:

⊚ SUBSTITUTE ANY OTHER FRUIT THAT IS IN SEASON.

Low-Fat Option:

⊚ USE LOW-FAT OR NON-FAT YOGURT.

In a big mixing bowl combine the oranges, bananas, mangoes, kiwifruit, pears, apples, melon and strawberries. Toss gently with lemon juice. Arrange the watercress on four salad plates. Starting with the bananas on the outside edge, arrange the fruit creatively while working towards the center of the plate.

In a blender or food processor blend the dressing ingredients. Pour the dressing over the fruit on the plate.

Mexican Pepper and Avocado Salad

SERVES 4–6

Today you can usually buy a variety of colorful sweet bell peppers. I occasionally serve this salad instead of vegetables as a side dish.

6	green onions, chopped
3	tomatoes, sliced into eighths (wedges)
2	sweet red peppers, cut in strips
1	sweet yellow or orange pepper, cut in strips
1	sweet green pepper, cut in strips
1 bunch	asparagus, steamed and halved crosswise
1 cup	cooked or canned red beans
1/2 cup	chopped fresh coriander
1/4 cup	chopped fresh parsley
2	avocados

DRESSING

4 cloves	garlic, minced
2 tbsp	sour cream
2 tbsp	lemon juice
2 tbsp	olive oil
1 tbsp	Dijon mustard
1/2 tsp	cayenne
	Salt and pepper to taste

In a salad bowl combine the green onions, tomatoes, peppers, asparagus, beans, coriander and parsley. Just before serving, slice the avocados and add to salad. In a small bowl whisk together the dressing ingredients. Pour over salad and toss well.

VARIATION:

- REPLACE ALL THE PEPPERS WITH ONE COLOR OF PEPPER. I WOULDN'T USE ONLY GREEN PEPPER AS THE SALAD MAY BE A LITTLE BITTER.

Low-Fat Options:

- USE A NON-FAT SOUR CREAM IN THE DRESSING.
- USE CANOLA OIL TO LOWER YOUR SATURATED FATS.

Pasta Salad with Caribbean Fruit and Vegetables

SERVES 4–6

A fresh pasta salad is a good way to use up leftover vegetables and fruit. The dressing that accompanies this salad can also be diluted with some juice or light soy sauce and used as a marinade.

4 cups	tricolored fusilli
4	celery stalks, chopped
4	carrots, halved lengthwise and sliced
2	oranges, peeled, seeded, quartered and halved crosswise
2	apples, chopped
I	small red onion, chopped
I	sweet red pepper, chopped
I	sweet green pepper, chopped
1/2 cup	cooked corn
1/2 cup	chopped fresh coriander

DRESSING

2 cloves	garlic, minced
I	mango, chopped
1/2 cup	orange juice or mango juice
1/3 cup	olive oil
1/4 cup	chopped fresh basil
2 tbsp	rice wine vinegar or red wine vinegar
I tbsp	lemon juice
1/2 tsp	salt
1/2 tsp	black pepper

In a large pot of boiling water cook pasta until tender but firm, about 12 minutes. Drain and return to pot. Add celery, carrots, oranges, apples, onion, peppers, corn and coriander; toss well. In a food processor purée all the dressing ingredients. Pour dressing over the salad and toss again. Chill 20 minutes before serving.

VARIATION:

◎ REPLACE THE MANGO WITH PAPAYA.

Sesame Grilled Vegetable Salad with Asiago Cheese

SERVES 4

This is a great starter salad or even a cold side dish. It's a good recipe for using up leftover vegetables.

1/4 cup	sesame oil
8	green onions
6	medium carrots, halved lengthwise and crosswise
4	large portobello mushrooms, quartered
4 cobs	corn, halved crosswise
2	medium zucchini, cut into strips
2	sweet red peppers, chopped
1	medium eggplant, sliced
1	fennel bulb, sliced lengthwise
2 cups	endive leaves
1 tbsp	sesame seeds
2 tbsp	balsamic vinegar
1/2 cup	shredded Asiago cheese

Brush sesame oil on all the vegetables. Grill the vegetables until tender but not overdone. Spread the endive evenly on a large platter and arrange the vegetables on top. Sprinkle with sesame seeds. Drizzle with balsamic vinegar. Sprinkle the Asiago cheese evenly over the vegetables.

VARIATION:

⊙ SUBSTITUTE OTHER FIRM VEGETABLES LIKE YAMS OR POTATOES, BUT MICROWAVE THEM BEFOREHAND TO START THEM COOKING.

Low-Fat Option:

⊙ LEAVE OUT THE ASIAGO CHEESE.

Chicken Salad with Pineapple and Coconut

SERVES 4

This chicken salad not only is a nice presentation but also has that Caribbean island flavor.

2	pineapples
4	celery stalks, chopped
2 cups	cubed cooked chicken
1/2 cup	raisins
1/2 cup	chopped fresh parsley
1/4 cup	walnuts, crushed
3 tbsp	unsweetened coconut flakes
2 tbsp	chopped fresh mint
1/2 tsp	cinnamon, for garnish

DRESSING

1/2 cup	plain or pineapple yogurt
2 tbsp	unsweetened coconut milk
1 tsp	Dijon mustard
1 tsp	balsamic vinegar
1/2 tsp	paprika
1/2 tsp	salt
1/2 tsp	black pepper

Slice the pineapples in half, scoop out the flesh and cut into cubes. Save the four shells to use as serving bowls. In a mixing bowl combine the pineapple, celery, chicken, raisins, parsley, walnuts, coconut and mint; mix well. In another bowl combine all the dressing ingredients and mix well. Toss salad with dressing and spoon into the pineapple shells. Garnish with a sprinkle of cinnamon.

VARIATION:

◉ REPLACE THE CHICKEN WITH SEAFOOD SUCH AS TUNA OR SHRIMP.

Low-Fat Option:

◉ USE LOW-FAT OR NON-FAT YOGURT.

Curry Caesar Salad with Grilled Chicken

SERVES 2–4

This is a popular dish for a main course or as a small starter.

2	boneless chicken breasts
	Juice of 1 lemon
1 tsp	garlic powder
1/2 tsp	salt
1/2 tsp	black pepper
1 tbsp	lemon rind
1	large head romaine lettuce
1 cup	toasted croutons
1/2 cup	freshly grated Parmesan cheese

DRESSING

4 cloves	garlic, chopped
1/3 cup	olive oil
1/3 cup	sour cream
2 tbsp	red wine vinegar
1 tbsp	chopped fresh coriander
1 tbsp	Dijon mustard
1 tbsp	lemon juice
1 tsp	mild curry powder or paste
1 tsp	Worcestershire sauce
1/2 tsp	anchovy paste

Coat the chicken with the lemon juice. Grill or broil chicken skin side down 3 minutes, then sprinkle with garlic powder, salt and pepper. Turn once and grill until the chicken is cooked through and has grill marks. Sprinkle with lemon rind towards the end of the grilling. Allow chicken to cool; slice into strips.

In a food processor combine all the dressing ingredients; blend well. Tear the lettuce into bite-size pieces; in a bowl, toss lettuce with dressing and croutons. Place the sliced chicken on top and sprinkle with Parmesan cheese.

VARIATION:

◉ REPLACE THE CHICKEN WITH TURKEY OR FISH.

Low-Fat Options:

◉ USE NON-FAT SOUR CREAM OR A LOW-FAT OR NON-FAT YOGURT.

◉ LEAVE OUT THE OLIVE OIL AND ADD 1/3 CUP LOW-FAT OR NON-FAT YOGURT.

◉ LEAVE OUT THE PARMESAN CHEESE.

Grilled Chicken Salad with Warm Spinach and Ginger

SERVES 2–4

This grilled chicken salad is not only a healthful meal or starter but also a vision to look at. I wanted a light lunch one day on the Century cruise ship and sampled a version of this warm salad.

2	boneless chicken breasts
2 tbsp	lemon juice
2 tbsp	liquid honey
1 tbsp	garlic powder
1/2 tsp	salt
1/2 tsp	black pepper
1 tbsp	olive oil
1 tsp	sesame oil
1 tsp	chopped fresh ginger
5 cups	spinach, cleaned and chopped
1 tsp	balsamic vinegar
1 tsp	Worcestershire sauce
1 tsp	sesame seeds

VARIATION:

⊘ REPLACE GINGER WITH GARLIC.

Low-Fat Options:

⊘ REPLACE CHICKEN WITH SWORDFISH OR LOW-CALORIE TOFU.

⊘ REPLACE THE OILS WITH 1/4 CUP OF VEGETABLE STOCK.

Coat the chicken breasts with lemon juice. Grill or broil chicken skin side down 3 minutes, then brush with honey and sprinkle with garlic powder, salt and pepper. Turn once and grill until the chicken is cooked through and has grill marks. Allow to cool; slice into strips.

Heat the olive and sesame oils in a wok. Add the ginger; toss for 1 minute. Add the spinach, balsamic vinegar, Worcestershire sauce, and salt and pepper to taste. Toss in wok 3 minutes or until spinach is cooked and wilted. Do not overcook. Arrange spinach on plates. Arrange chicken over spinach and sprinkle with sesame seeds.

Cold Beef and Orange Salad on Watercress

SERVES 4

The combination of citrus and beef in a salad creates a very light flavor that is reminiscent of the Caribbean.

1	8–10-oz sirloin steak
1/2 cup	orange juice, pulp included
1/2 cup	light soy sauce
2 cloves	garlic, finely chopped
2 tbsp	orange rind
1 tsp	hot horseradish
1/2 tsp	dried thyme
1/2 tsp	dried oregano
1/2 tsp	black pepper
2	large seedless oranges, thickly sliced crosswise
4 cups	watercress
8	cherry tomatoes, halved

DRESSING

1/4 cup	orange juice
2 tbsp	olive oil
1 tbsp	orange rind
1 tsp	balsamic vinegar
1 tsp	Worcestershire sauce
1 tsp	Dijon mustard
1/2 tsp	black pepper
2 cloves	garlic, minced

VARIATIONS:

- REPLACE DRIED THYME AND OREGANO WITH OTHER DRIED HERBS SUCH AS BASIL, MINT OR ROSEMARY.

- ADD A LITTLE CURRY POWDER TO THE MARINADE OR DRESSING.

Low-Fat Option:

- USE CHICKEN OR TURKEY BREAST INSTEAD OF BEEF.

Trim the fat off the steak. In a bowl whisk together the orange juice, soy sauce, garlic, orange rind, horseradish, thyme, oregano and pepper. Set aside 3 tbsp of the marinade. Marinate beef, covered and refrigerated, for at least 2 hours. Grill or broil the steak 8 minutes for rare and 15 minutes for well-done, occasionally basting with the reserved marinade. Grill or broil the orange slices until browned. Let steak and orange cool.

Meanwhile, combine all the dressing ingredients in a blender and blend well. Slice beef and serve on a bed of watercress with tomatoes and grilled oranges. Drizzle the dressing over the salad.

Arhawak Salad

SERVES 4

This salad was one of my favorites in the Caribbean. It was impressive visually but amazingly easy to prepare.

2 tsp	curry powder
	Thinly sliced white cabbage
4 handfuls	mixed salads
4	mangoes, sliced
2	avocados, sliced
2	boiled lobsters, chilled and halved (optional)
8	cooked small shrimp
	Juice of 2 limes
	French dressing to taste

To a large pot of boiling water add the curry and cabbage; cook until cabbage has softened. Drain, refresh under cold water, drain again and chill. On each plate of mixed salads, arrange slices of mango and avocado. Place half a boiled lobster, if using, on each plate. Sprinkle with the shrimp and cabbage. Stir together lime juice and French dressing. Drizzle dressing over salad.

Recipe from L'Arhawak (Marigot), St. Martin.

Lemon Swordfish Salad

SERVES 4

The charm of this recipe is that it can be prepared as a warm or cold salad. I occasionally serve it as a main course for lunch.

2 tbsp	light soy sauce
2 tbsp	lemon juice
1 tbsp	lemon rind
1 tbsp	liquid honey
1 tsp	sesame oil
1/2 tsp	black pepper
1/4 tsp	salt
2	small swordfish steaks OR 1 large steak, halved

SALAD

1 head	Boston lettuce
1 head	endive
8	cherry tomatoes, halved
1 tbsp	lemon rind
1 tsp	sesame seeds, for garnish

DRESSING

1 tbsp	balsamic vinegar
1 tbsp	orange juice
1 tbsp	lemon juice
1 tsp	sesame oil

In a small mixing bowl whisk together the soy sauce, lemon juice, lemon rind, honey, sesame oil, pepper and salt. Brush the marinade on both sides of the swordfish and grill about 4 minutes on each side. Let the swordfish cool, if desired. Tear the lettuce and endive into bite-size pieces and place in a salad bowl with the tomatoes and lemon rind. Whisk together the dressing ingredients. Slice the swordfish against the grain and toss it with the salad. Pour the dressing over the salad and garnish with sesame seeds.

VARIATION:

⊘ REPLACE THE SWORDFISH WITH GRILLED TUNA OR CHICKEN.

Pizzas, Pasta and Grains

Basic Pizza

MAKES ONE 8–10-INCH PIZZA

The island of Cozumel, near the tip of Mexico's Yucatan Peninsula, is encircled by coral reefs, making it one of the world's top diving destinations. What could be nicer, after a day underwater, than to visit Pizza Rolandi and sample one of the best pizzas I have recently experienced. They use all fresh ingredients as well as their imagination for the toppings. Here is one you can experiment with.

1/4 lb	pizza dough or French bread dough
1/2 cup	tomato pizza sauce OR 1/4 cup chopped tomatoes and 1/4 cup tomato paste seasoned with oregano and olive oil
1/4 lb	shredded oaxaca or mozzarella cheese

On a lightly floured surface, roll out the pizza dough into an 8–10-inch circle. Spread the tomato sauce evenly over the crust. Sprinkle with cheese. Slide pizza onto a pizza stone or greased baking sheet. Set rack in lower third of oven. Bake at 450°F until the cheese is melted and the crust is crispy.

VARIATIONS:

⊙ REPLACE THE TOMATO SAUCE WITH PESTO.

⊙ ADD YOUR VEGETABLE OR CHICKEN LEFTOVERS TO THIS BASIC PIZZA.

Low-Fat Option:

⊙ USE A CHEESE SUCH AS LOW-FAT MOZZARELLA.

⊙ *Recipe from Pizza Rolandi, Cozumel, Mexico.*

The Island Breakfast Pizza

MAKES ONE 12-INCH PIZZA

Breakfast is the first meal we eat in the day, and so we are breaking the night's fasting. The word was first recorded in the fifteenth century, when "breaking one's fast" became "breakfast." I can't think of a better way to end the night's denial of food than with a morning feast of Island Breakfast Pizza. I sampled it onboard the Century cruise ship, and it not only awakened me, it had my taste buds dancing!

4	eggs, gently scrambled
I	12-inch pizza crust OR focaccia bread
4	eggs, gently scrambled
4	slices of bacon, cooked but not crisp, chopped
2	medium breakfast sausages, cooked and sliced
1/2 cup	shredded Cheddar cheese
I	small red onion, thinly sliced
1/4 tsp	dried rosemary
1/4 tsp	dried thyme
	Salt and pepper to taste

Spread scrambled eggs evenly over pizza crust or focaccia. Arrange bacon and sausage over eggs. Sprinkle the pizza with the cheese, onion, rosemary, thyme, salt and pepper. Bake on nonstick or greased cookie sheet at 350°F for 8–10 minutes, until the cheese is melted.

VARIATION:

◎ REPLACE THE BACON AND SAUSAGE WITH 1/2 LB COOKED GROUND TURKEY, BEEF OR CHICKEN, AND ADD SOME GRAVY.

Low-Fat Option:

◎ LEAVE OUT THE MEAT AND ADD VEGETABLES; TRY SWEET RED PEPPER AND MUSHROOMS.

TIP:

◎ USE A COMMERCIAL "TEA BISCUIT" MIX FOR YOUR CRUST INSTEAD OF A STANDARD PIZZA SHELL OR FOCACCIA BREAD. FOLLOW PACKAGE DIRECTIONS FOR BAKING THE TEA BISCUIT SHELL.

Vegetarian "Rajas" Pizza
MAKES ONE 8–10-INCH PIZZA

St. Miguel is Cozumel's only town. It is easy to negotiate on foot, for many downtown streets are closed to traffic. The island's hub is a conglomeration of budget hotels, businesses, shops, nightspots and restaurants, like Pizza Rolandi. This pizza recipe ("rajas" means strips) is a delicious classic combination of roasted mild poblano chiles with creamed corn and onions. Any leftover rajas makes a great taco or crêpe stuffing. My friend Carlos, from Michael's cigar lounge on the Century, recommends this pizza.

I	basic pizza (recipe on page 68)
I oz	blue cheese, crumbled
1/2 cup	rajas (recipe follows)

Prepare the basic pizza. Top tomato sauce with rajas and sprinkle with blue cheese. Bake at 450°F until cheese is melted and crust is crispy.

RAJAS (makes 1/2 cup)

I tsp	butter
1/2	small onion, thinly sliced
I	large poblano or Anaheim chile, roasted, peeled and seeded
1/3 cup	cooked corn
1/3 cup	whipping cream
	Salt to taste

In a medium skillet melt the butter. Sauté the onion until translucent but not brown. Add chile, corn and cream. Cook until cream is reduced by half and has a green tinge. Stir in salt.

VARIATION:

⊚ REPLACE THE BLUE CHEESE WITH STILTON.

Low-Fat Options:

⊚ USE LOW-FAT MOZZARELLA CHEESE.

⊚ REPLACE THE WHIPPING CREAM WITH HALF-AND-HALF CREAM.

TIP:

⊚ ROAST THE ANAHEIM CHILE ON A GREASED COOKIE SHEET UNTIL SKIN IS BLACKENED SOMEWHAT. CUT LENGTHWISE AND DISCARD SEEDS INSIDE. PEEL SHOULD SLIDE OFF.

⊚ *Recipe from Pizza Rolandi, Cozumel, Mexico.*

Mexican Veggie Pizza
MAKES ONE 8–10-INCH PIZZA

A visit to Museo de la Isla de Cozumel (Museum of the Island of Cozumel) will steep you in the island's history, from its reputation as a revered Maya religious destination down through the ages of trading and battle. Sustain the Mexican mood at dinner by ordering Pizza Rolandi's Mexican Veggie Pizza—a Mayan twist to Italian dough. Or make it at home and let your imagination take you there. Use the vegetables you are most fond of.

1	basic pizza (recipe on page 68)
1/4 cup	*chaya* or spinach, blanched and chopped
1/4 cup	*chayote* or zucchini, blanched and diced
1	small jalapeño pepper, sliced
1	plum tomato, sliced
2	sun-dried tomatoes, chopped
1/2	small avocado, sliced

Prepare the basic pizza. Top tomato sauce with *chaya*, *chayote*, jalapeño pepper, plum tomato and sun-dried tomatoes. Sprinkle with cheese. Bake at 450°F until cheese is melted and crust is crispy. Before serving, garnish with sliced avocado.

VARIATION:

⊕ FOR A COMPLETE VEGETARIAN MEAL USE A CHEESE SUBSTITUTE SUCH AS GRATED SOY CHEESE.

Low-Fat Option:

⊕ REPLACE THE CHEESE WITH LOW-FAT MOZZARELLA OR CALORIE-REDUCED GOAT CHEESE.

⊕ *Recipe from Pizza Rolandi, Cozumel, Mexico.*

Deep-Dish Vegetable Pizza on Focaccia

SERVES 3-4

Related to pizza and calzone, focaccia is flat bread simply made with flour, water, yeast, and a little oil for flavor and handling. For years, the only place in North America where you could get focaccia—they called it Genoese flat bread—was in San Francisco. Toppings on focaccia are normally to flavor and enhance the bread and are never applied as generously as are toppings for pizza, but I have taken the liberty here to use it as a more subtle base for this tasty Carib-style deep-dish pizza.

1	large flavored or unflavored focaccia loaf
3 tbsp	Caribbean Chili Sauce (page 6), Creole Sauce (page 7) or Homemade Barbecue Sauce (page 10)
2	medium carrots, cut into thin strips
1	medium red onion, cut into thin strips
1	small eggplant, thinly sliced
1	small zucchini, cut into thin strips
1	sweet red pepper, cut into rings
1 cup	finely chopped broccoli
3/4 cup	crumbled mild goat cheese
1/4 cup	freshly grated Parmesan cheese

Place the focaccia bread on a baking sheet. (If the bread is a little thick, place another baking sheet on top and press down to flatten it. Be careful not to break or crack the bread.) Spread sauce on the bread and arrange vegetables on top. Sprinkle with goat cheese and Parmesan. Bake at 400°F for 10–12 minutes or until cheese starts to bubble and turn brown.

VARIATIONS:

○ REPLACE THE GOAT CHEESE WITH MOZZARELLA.

○ REPLACE ANY OF THE VEGETABLES WITH LEFTOVER VEGETABLES OR WITH YOUR FAVORITES.

○ REPLACE SOME OF THE VEGETABLES WITH SEAFOOD OR MEAT, LIKE PEPPERONI OR SAUSAGE.

Low-Fat Option:

○ LEAVE OUT THE CHEESE OR USE LOW-FAT CHEESE. YOU CAN PURCHASE A GOAT CHEESE THAT HAS THE TEXTURE OF MOZZARELLA BUT LESS FAT.

Cajun Pizza with Leftovers

MAKES ONE 12-INCH PIZZA

Pizza is a hit all over North America, though its origins date back to Naples in the sixteenth century, when King Ferdinand, its biggest fan, commissioned a famous Italian pizza chef to supply his court with the circular sensation. A good thing never stays put, and during World War II, soldiers returning home from Italy brought the recipe back with them. Wait until you taste my special Cajun concoction—and you get to use up your leftovers!

1	large pizza shell, or thinner focaccia bread
	Creole Sauce (recipe on page 7)
1 cup	cubed cooked chicken or turkey or cooked ground meat
	Cooked carrots
	Cooked asparagus
1/2 cup	sliced button mushrooms
1 cup	combined shredded mozzarella and swiss cheese
1/2 tsp	black pepper
1/2 tsp	dried oregano
1/4 tsp	dried sage
1/2 tsp	Dry Jerk Seasoning (recipe on page 4) (optional)

Brush pizza shell with Creole Sauce. Sprinkle with the chicken and arrange carrots, asparagus and mushrooms on top (cut them differently for interest). Sprinkle with cheese, black pepper, oregano and sage. If using Dry Jerk Seasoning, sprinkle it on last. Bake pizza at 350°F for 10 minutes or until cheese bubbles.

VARIATION:

⊚ REPLACE THE CREOLE SAUCE WITH HOMEMADE BARBECUE SAUCE (RECIPE ON PAGE 10).

Low-Fat Option:

⊚ USE A COMBINATION OF LOWER-FAT CHEESES.

Seafood Black Pizza
MAKES ONE 8–10-INCH PIZZA

Unless you're a mycologist or you take one with you, don't go picking mushrooms to eat. Of the many thousands of fungi, only a handful are edible. One mushroom delicacy is **huitlacoche**, a black mushroom that grows on corn. Fortunately, you can buy it already cooked in small cans at specialty stores. It contrasts beautifully with the shrimp and onions in this recipe from Cozumel's Pizza Rolandi, but you can substitute without seriously affecting the taste.

I	Basic Pizza (recipe on page 68)
I tsp	olive oil
7	tiger shrimp, peeled
1/4 cup	canned *huitlacoche* (black mushrooms), drained OR 1/2 cup chopped shiitake or portobello mushrooms
1/4 cup	thinly sliced red onion
I tbsp	chopped fresh basil

Prepare the basic pizza. In a small skillet heat the oil. Sauté the shrimp until just cooked through, about 4 minutes. Top tomato sauce with *huitlacoche*, onion, shrimp and basil. Sprinkle with cheese. Bake at 450°F until cheese is melted and crust is crispy.

VARIATION:

◉ REPLACE THE SHRIMP WITH I CUP OF LARGE SCALLOPS.

Low-Fat Option:

◉ USE LOW-FAT MOZZARELLA.

◉ *Recipe from Pizza Rolandi, Cozumel, Mexico.*

Charro Pizza
MAKES ONE 8–10-INCH PIZZA

South of San Miguel on Mexico's Cozumel Island is Parque Laguna de Chancanaab. Surrounding the lagoon is a shady botanical garden with hundreds of tropical and sub-tropical plants. You may never go to Cozumel, but recipes like this one from Pizza Rolandi bring the flavor of Mexico right into your home. Here, I substituted the ever-popular refried beans for the tomato sauce, which helps make it a **charro**, or "flashy," pizza!

1/4 lb	pizza dough or French bread dough
1/2 cup	Traditional Refried Beans (recipe below)
1/4 lb	shredded oaxaca or mozzarella cheese
1	banana pepper, roasted, peeled and seeded OR 1 serrano chile, chopped
2 oz	chorizo sausage, fried and chopped
1/4 cup	chopped red onion

Low-Fat Options:

- USE LOW-FAT MOZZARELLA.
- REPLACE THE REFRIED BEANS WITH TOMATO SAUCE.
- USE VEGETABLE OIL INSTEAD OF BACON.

On a lightly floured surface, roll out the pizza dough into an 8–10-inch circle. Spread the refried beans on the crust. Sprinkle with cheese, pepper, chorizo and onion. Bake at 450°F until cheese is melted and crust is crispy.

TRADITIONAL REFRIED BEANS (makes 1/2 cup)

1 tbsp	chopped bacon
3 tbsp	chopped onion
1/2 tsp	chopped jalapeño or serrano pepper
1-1/2 cups	cooked black beans, mashed

In a medium skillet fry the bacon until crisp. Remove the bacon. Add the onion and sauté, stirring, until translucent but not brown. Return bacon to pan. Add the pepper and beans; continue to cook, stirring, until thick.

- *Recipe from Pizza Rolandi, Cozumel, Mexico.*

Mexican Pita

SERVES 2–4

In the Arab world, a meal without meat is conceivable, but a meal without bread is unthinkable. Most Arab bread is made from wheat flour that has been lightly leavened and shaped into a hollow flat round, forming a pocket that is perfect for stuffing. I had this in Mexico using the Chili Sauce. Wow!

1	large pita or 2 small pitas
2 tbsp	Caribbean Chili Sauce (recipe on page 6)
1	small red onion, sliced into thin rings
1 cup	broken feta cheese
1/2 cup	cooked red kidney beans
1 tbsp	chopped pitted black olives
1 tbsp	chopped fresh rosemary
1/2 tsp	black pepper

Brush pita with sauce. Arrange the ingredients on the shell. Transfer to a baking sheet and bake at 350°F for 10–12 minutes. Be careful not to burn the pita or ingredients.

VARIATION:

◎ REPLACE THE FETA CHEESE WITH A MILD GOAT CHEESE.

Low-Fat Option:

◎ REPLACE THE OLIVES WITH CHOPPED MUSHROOMS.

Fettuccine with Island Spices and Herbs in Chicken Cream Sauce

SERVES 4

This is a great way to perk up leftover chicken and vegetables, adding zest with the island spices and tossing it with fettuccine, all elegantly bathed in a delicate cream sauce. This recipe will win approval at any dinner party.

1 tbsp	olive oil
1/2 cup	pearl onions, sliced
2	celery stalks, chopped
1	sweet green pepper, diced
1 cup	cubed cooked chicken
1 cup	frozen peas
1/4 cup	chopped fresh basil
1 tbsp	chopped fresh thyme
1/4 tsp	cinnamon
1/4 tsp	ground nutmeg
1/4 cup	dry white wine
1 cup	table cream
1	bay leaf
	Salt and pepper to taste
1/2 cup	crumbled goat cheese
3 cups	cooked fettuccine
1/4 cup	freshly grated Parmesan cheese

VARIATION:

⊚ REPLACE THE CHICKEN WITH LEFTOVER TURKEY.

Low-Fat Option:

⊚ USE LOW-FAT OR NON-FAT SOUR CREAM INSTEAD OF THE TABLE CREAM.

In a large deep sauté pan or skillet heat the oil; sauté the pearl onions 2 minutes or until translucent. Add the celery and green pepper. Add the chicken, peas, basil, thyme, cinnamon, nutmeg and white wine. Allow to thicken; add the cream, bay leaf, salt and pepper. Allow to reduce; discard bay leaf. Gently stir in the goat cheese. Add the cooked fettuccine and toss to coat well. Sprinkle with Parmesan cheese.

Penne with Bacon and Sausage in Spicy Tomato Sauce

SERVES 4

Just as Mexican food has been adopted into the cuisine of the world, other national cuisines can be mixed with Mexican dishes to create exciting new international blends, combining the tastes and textures of both, or several. This recipe uses Mexican spices tossed with penne noodles to produce an enticing, spicy pasta.

1 tbsp	olive oil
3	hot Italian sausages
1/2 lb	lean bacon, chopped
1	medium onion, chopped
4 cloves	garlic, finely chopped
2	celery stalks, chopped
2	carrots, shaved
1 can	stewed tomatoes (19 oz/540 mL)
1/2 cup	dry red wine
1 tbsp	tomato paste
1 tsp	chili powder
1/2 tsp	dried basil
1/2 tsp	dried oregano
1/2 tsp	dried sage
1/2 tsp	hot pepper sauce
1	bay leaf
	Salt and pepper to taste
4 cups	cooked penne

VARIATION:

◉ REPLACE THE ITALIAN SAUSAGE WITH OTHER TYPES OF SAUSAGE.

Low-Fat Options:

◉ LEAVE OUT THE BACON.

◉ BUY AN ITALIAN SAUSAGE LOWER IN FAT.

In a deep sauté pan or skillet heat the oil; sauté the sausages on all sides until cooked through. Remove from pan. Gently brown the bacon, but do not burn. Meanwhile, slice sausages into bite-size pieces. To the bacon add the onion, garlic, celery and carrots; sauté for 2 minutes. Add sausage, tomatoes, red wine, tomato paste, chili powder, basil, oregano, sage, hot pepper sauce, bay leaf, salt and pepper. Simmer, stirring occasionally, for 10 minutes, adding more wine if sauce reduces too much. Discard the bay leaf. Combine sauce with the penne and mix well.

Penne with Grilled Vegetables

SERVES 4–6

Authentic Mexican food has many influences—Indian, Spanish, French, Moorish, and even Chinese. Contrary to common belief, it is not always hotly spiced. Corn is the country's greatest contribution to global cookery, but the list also includes tomatoes, avocados, squashes, pumpkin and chilies. Grilled vegetables are a very large part of the Mexican diet. For this dish, I've combined grilled vegetables with pasta. Try it—you'll soon be using grilled vegetables with everything!

4 cups	cooked penne

MARINADE

1/4 cup	vegetable stock
1 tbsp	chopped fresh basil
1 tbsp	chopped fresh thyme
1 tbsp	light soy sauce
1/2 tsp	black pepper
1/2 tsp	balsamic vinegar

VEGETABLES

1 cup	broccoli florets
6	asparagus spears
4	large carrots, julienned
1	zucchini, julienned
1	portobello mushroom

SPICY TOMATO SAUCE

1 tbsp	olive oil
1	medium red onion OR 2 shallots, chopped
4 cloves	garlic, finely chopped
1 can	stewed tomatoes (19 oz/540 mL)
2	jalapeño peppers, chopped
1/4 cup	chopped fresh basil
1 tbsp	sugar or liquid honey
1 tsp	black pepper
1/2 tsp	salt
1	bay leaf

VARIATION:

◎ REPLACE ANY VEGETABLE WITH OTHERS THAT ARE FIRM AND WILL GRILL NICELY SUCH AS CAULIFLOWER OR EGGPLANT.

Low-Fat Option:

◎ SAUTÉ THE ONION AND GARLIC IN 1/4 CUP OF VEGETABLE STOCK INSTEAD OF OLIVE OIL.

Health Option:

◎ REPLACE THE SUGAR OR HONEY WITH A CALORIE-REDUCED LIQUID SWEETENER.

In a large mixing bowl combine the marinade ingredients. Add the vegetables to the marinade, stirring to coat well and marinate for 1/2 hour. Grill vegetables until tender but not overdone.

SAUCE

In a medium saucepan heat the oil; sauté the onion and garlic for 2 minutes or until translucent. Stir in the tomatoes, jalapeño peppers, basil, sugar, black pepper, salt and bay leaf; simmer, stirring occasionally, for 8–10 minutes. Discard the bay leaf. Spoon the sauce over the penne and top with the grilled vegetables.

Red Pepper and Clams with Spaghetti

SERVES 4–6

After a hard day this recipe will bring you back to life.

1/2 cup	chicken stock
1	medium red onion, chopped
2 cloves	garlic, chopped
1/4 cup	chopped fresh basil
2	sweet red peppers, seeded and diced
1/4 cup	dry white wine
1 cup	rinsed canned clams
1/2 cup	chopped fresh parsley
1/2 tsp	salt
1/2 tsp	black pepper
3 cups	cooked spaghetti
1/4 cup	freshly grated Parmesan cheese

In a large saucepan heat the chicken stock; sauté the onion on high heat about 3 minutes or until translucent. Add the garlic, basil, red peppers, and white wine, and sauté another 3 minutes on medium heat. Then add the clams, parsley, salt and pepper.

Add the spaghetti to the saucepan and mix well, about 2 minutes. If the sauce needs more liquid, add more soup stock. Sprinkle with Parmesan cheese before serving.

VARIATION:

◉ SUBSTITUTE SHRIMP OR I CAN OF FLAKED TUNA OR SALMON FOR CLAMS.

Health Option:

◉ LEAVE OUT THE WHITE WINE.

Saffron Rice

SERVES 4

Saffron, the most expensive spice in the world, is worth far more than its weight in gold. More than a quarter of a million crocus flowers must be harvested to obtain just one pound of saffron, and the three stigmas from each crocus must be collected by hand. Fortunately, very little saffron is needed in most dishes, sometimes as little as a pinch, as in this recipe from Kelly's Caribbean Bar, Grill and Brewery in Key West, Florida.

2 cups	water
1 cup	chicken stock
1/2 tsp	saffron
1/2 tsp	turmeric
1-1/2 cups	long-grain white rice
	Salt and pepper to taste

In a large pot bring water, chicken stock, saffron and turmeric to a boil. Add rice; cover and simmer about 20 minutes. Add salt and pepper to taste.

☺ *Recipe from Kelly's Caribbean Bar, Grill and Brewery, Key West, Florida.*

Vegetarian

West Indian Vegetable Stew

SERVES 4–6

In the nineteenth century, Ceylonese immigrant workers brought their cuisine to the West Indies, and it soon became popular with the inhabitants. Naturally, the blend of nearly 20 spices called curry was a critical part of their recipes. I don't use such a fiery hot curry for my West Indian Vegetable Stew—you'll find my version a zesty yet delicate combination of flavors. Occasionally, I add cubed tofu or a can of kidney beans. Served with basmati rice—with a cubed banana in it—this makes a perfect meal.

3 cups	vegetable stock
1/2 cup	dry white wine (optional)
2	potatoes, cubed
2	carrots, diced
1	red onion, chopped
1	bay leaf
1 cup	non-fat yogurt
1/2 cup	chopped fresh coriander
1 tbsp	mild curry powder
1 tbsp	liquid honey or brown sugar
	Salt and black pepper to taste
1 cup	cubed eggplant
1/2 cup	chopped green onions
1/2 cup	raisins
6	asparagus spears, chopped
2	tomatoes, diced
1	fennel bulb, chopped
1 cup	broccoli (florets)
1/2	cauliflower, chopped

VARIATION:

◎ FOR A NON-VEGETARIAN STEW, ADD 4 PRE-COOKED BONELESS CHICKEN BREASTS, CUBED.

Health Options:

◎ LEAVE OUT THE WHITE WINE.

◎ REPLACE THE HONEY WITH CALORIE-REDUCED LIQUID SWEETENER.

In a medium saucepan bring to a boil 1/2 cup of the vegetable stock, wine (if using), potatoes, carrots, red onion and bay leaf. Reduce heat and simmer, adding more stock if necessary, 8–10 minutes or until vegetables are tender. Add the remaining stock, yogurt, coriander, curry powder, honey, salt and pepper, stirring until smooth. Add the eggplant, green onions, raisins, asparagus, tomatoes, fennel, broccoli and cauliflower; cook another 12–15 minutes until vegetables are tender. Do not overcook. Discard the bay leaf. A side dish of pita bread with olives and sun-dried tomatoes is an excellent accompaniment to this stew.

Island Medley of Vegetables
SERVES 4–6

In San Juan, I sampled a version of this Island Medley of Vegetables. You can add your own favorite vegetables, and it is a great recipe for using up leftovers. I serve this meal with pasta or rice.

3 cups	vegetable stock
1/2 cup	chopped fresh basil
1/2 cup	dry red wine
1/4 cup	chopped fresh dill
1 tsp	black pepper
1/2 tsp	salt
1/2 tsp	cinnamon
1/4 tsp	ground cloves
1/4 tsp	ground nutmeg
4 cloves	garlic, crushed
2	bay leaves
2 cups	cubed butternut squash
2	large potatoes, cubed
2	large carrots, cubed
1 cup	broccoli florets
1 cup	cauliflower florets
2	sweet green peppers, chopped
1	zucchini, cubed
1	large red onion, chopped

In a large soup pot combine the stock, basil, red wine, dill, black pepper, salt, cinnamon, cloves, nutmeg, garlic and bay leaves; bring to a boil. Reduce heat and add squash, potatoes and carrot; simmer until vegetables are almost done. Stir in the broccoli, cauliflower, green peppers, zucchini and red onion; simmer another 5–8 minutes, until vegetables are tender but not soft. Discard the bay leaves.

VARIATION:

⊚ ADD CHICKEN OR BEEF. I HAVE ADDED TOFU AND SWORDFISH. EXPERIMENT!

Low-Fat Option:

⊚ THIS IS A FAIRLY LOW-FAT MEAL ALREADY!

Poached Salmon in Pineapple (page 113). *Linda Corbett, food styled by Johanna Weinstein*

Caribbean Vegetable Stew

SERVES 4–6

Take the freshest vegetables and create a hearty stew. Have fun experimenting.

1 tbsp	vegetable oil
1	large red onion, quartered
4 cloves	garlic, minced
1 cup	vegetable stock
4	celery stalks, chopped
1 tsp	balsamic vinegar
1 tsp	Worcestershire sauce
1 tbsp	mild curry powder (optional)
1 tsp	dried basil
1 tsp	dried rosemary
1 tsp	paprika
1 tsp	chili powder
1/2 tsp	cayenne
1	bay leaf
6	medium potatoes, cubed
4	large carrots, chopped
1	large sweet potato, peeled and cubed
1	fennel bulb, sliced
1/2 cup	dry red wine
4	medium tomatoes, chopped
2	zucchini, chopped
1/2 tsp	each salt and black pepper

In a large soup pot heat the oil; sauté the onion, garlic and celery until onion is translucent. Add vegetable stock, balsamic vinegar, Worcestershire sauce, curry power (if using), basil, rosemary, paprika, chili powder, cayenne and bay leaf; bring to a boil. Add potatoes, carrots, sweet potato and fennel; simmer 15 minutes. Add red wine, tomatoes and zucchini; simmer another 5 minutes. Vegetables should be tender but not over-cooked. Season with salt and pepper. Discard bay leaf.

VARIATION:

⊚ SUBSTITUTE SOME CUBED FIRM TOFU FOR SOME OF THE POTATOES.

Low-Fat Option:

⊚ SAUTÉ IN VEGETABLE STOCK RATHER THAN IN OIL.

Health Option:

⊚ SAUTÉ IN VEGETABLE STOCK RATHER THAN IN OIL.

Chicken with Sautéed Vegetables and Raisins (page 131). *Linda Corbett, food styled by Johanna Weinstein*

Vegetarian Bean Stew
SERVES 6

The word "stew" was first recorded in the fifteenth century and it meant, literally, to take a steam bath. And, sure enough, your vegetables will indeed take a bath, but not a long one. Then you'll use the classic Cantonese method of cooking and stir-fry all of these delightful vegetables. The combination of gentle boiling and stir-frying will render this vegetarian mélange a one-pot perfection!

2	small potatoes, cubed
2	carrots, sliced lengthwise
2 tbsp	vegetable oil
4 cloves	garlic, chopped
4	celery stalks, sliced diagonally
3	small jalapeño peppers, chopped
2	tomatoes, cut into wedges
1	sweet red pepper, sliced
1	small cabbage, cut into wedges
1	bunch green onions, sliced diagonally
2 cups	vegetable stock
1 can	red kidney beans (28 oz/796 mL)
1 tsp	dried basil
1 tbsp	chili powder
1/2 tsp	dried thyme
1 tsp	black pepper
1/2 tsp	salt

VARIATION:

⊚ REPLACE ANY OF THE VEGETABLES WITH OTHERS AND EXPERIMENT BY ADDING OTHER DRY HERBS SUCH AS OREGANO OR ROSEMARY, OR A COMBINATION.

Low-Fat Option:

⊚ SAUTÉ THE VEGETABLES IN 1/4 CUP OF LOW-SODIUM VEGETABLE STOCK.

Boil potatoes until they are almost tender and then add the carrots; boil until carrots are tender. Drain. In a wok or large skillet heat the oil. Add the garlic, celery, jalapeño peppers, tomatoes, red pepper, cabbage, and green onions; stir-fry until tender but not overcooked. Add the vegetable stock, red kidney beans, potato, carrot, basil, chili powder and thyme. Steam the vegetables for a couple of minutes, being careful not to overcook them. Season with pepper and salt.

Ken's Egg Zucchini Pie

SERVES 4

Squashes, of which zucchini is a summer variety, are exclusively North American in origin. No references to squashes or pumpkin have ever been found in any ancient writings, nor have they been found growing wild in any other part of the world. When I was in Jamaica I was served a version of this recipe that had a mild touch of curry added, but you decide if you want to "Carib-ize" with island spices or not.

2	large zucchini, sliced
1 tbsp	all-purpose flour
1 tbsp	olive oil
2 cloves	garlic, finely chopped
6	eggs
1/2 cup	finely shredded carrot
1/2 cup	cottage cheese
1/2 tsp	dried oregano
1/2 tsp	dried basil
1/2 tsp	mild curry powder (optional)
1/2 cup	shredded mozzarella cheese
1/4 cup	freshly grated Parmesan cheese

In a bowl toss the zucchini with the flour to coat well. In a large skillet heat the oil; sauté the garlic for 2 minutes. Add the zucchini and gently fry for 2 minutes or until tender. Drain on paper towels. In a mixing bowl lightly beat the eggs. Stir in the carrot, cottage cheese, oregano, basil and curry powder (if using). Pour the egg mixture into a 12-inch pie plate and arrange the zucchini slices on top. Sprinkle with mozzarella and Parmesan cheese. Bake at 350°F for 25 minutes or until pie is firm. Let cool for 5 minutes before serving.

VARIATION:

◎ REPLACE THE ZUCCHINI WITH EGGPLANT—IT WORKS REALLY WELL.

Low-Fat Options:

◎ USE A LOW-FAT CHEESE OR GOAT CHEESE.

◎ USE A LOW-FAT COTTAGE CHEESE.

◎ USE LIQUID EGG SUBSTITUTE.

Mexican Vegetarian Chili
SERVES 6

Chili powder is a blend of spices created in the American Southwest during the nineteenth century. It is generally a blend of red (cayenne) pepper, cumin, oregano, salt and garlic pepper. The bite comes from capsaicin, the most pungent naturally produced chemical in cayenne peppers. This vegetarian chili is one of my favorite recipes from the Caribbean. I developed it to have an abundance of flavor, sometimes adding cubed tofu. You can serve this on basmati rice or even on toast.

2 tbsp	olive oil
2	medium onions, chopped
4 cloves	garlic, chopped
4	celery stalks, chopped
4	carrots, chopped
1	sweet red pepper, chopped
1	sweet green pepper, chopped
1	jalapeño pepper, chopped (2 if you're brave)
1 cup	chopped purple cabbage
1 can	stewed tomatoes (28 oz/796 mL)
1	bay leaf
2 cups	vegetable stock
1 cup	cooked red kidney beans
1 cup	apple juice
1/2 cup	dry red wine (optional)
3 tbsp	chili powder
1 tbsp	lemon juice
1/4 cup	chopped fresh coriander
1/4 cup	chopped fresh mint
1/4 cup	chopped fresh basil
2	avocados, cubed (optional)
1 tbsp	chopped chives for garnish

VARIATIONS:

◎ ADD CUBED TOFU.

◎ ADD LEFTOVER VEGETABLES.

◎ REPLACE THE FRESH HERBS WITH DRIED ONES (USE 1/2 TSP EACH INSTEAD).

Low-Fat Options:

◎ SAUTÉ IN 1/4 CUP VEGETABLE STOCK RATHER THAN OIL.

◎ LEAVE OUT THE RED WINE.

In a large soup pot heat the oil; sauté the onions and garlic for 3 minutes. Add the celery, carrots, red and green peppers, jalapeño pepper and cabbage; sauté another 3 minutes. Add tomatoes, bay leaf, vegetable stock, kidney beans, apple juice, red wine (if using), chili powder and lemon juice. Add the coriander, mint, basil and avocado (if using), 5 minutes before serving. Discard the bay leaf. Garnish each bowl of chili with freshly chopped chives. (You may also add crushed tortilla chips for garnish.)

Sesame Grilled Portobello Mushrooms

SERVES 4

Sesame oil is a key ingredient in Asian cookery. Of the two types, the darker variety has an extremely strong flavor and aroma. A few drops will transform the blandest food. Mingled with the wonderful flavor of grilled mushrooms on top of garlic mashed potatoes with a pinch of curry powder mixed in—get ready for a treat!

2 cloves	garlic, crushed
2 tbsp	sesame oil
2 tbsp	olive oil
1 tbsp	light soy sauce
1 tsp	Dijon mustard
1/4 tsp	dried basil
4	large portobello mushrooms (or 8 medium), stems removed
1 tbsp	toasted sesame seeds for garnish

In a small bowl whisk together the garlic, sesame oil, olive oil, soy sauce, mustard and basil. Gently brush the mixture over the mushrooms. Grill the mushrooms for 2 minutes on each side or until grill marks appear. On a cookie sheet, toast the sesame seeds at 350°F, until brown. Garnish the grilled mushrooms with the toasted sesame seeds. Serve with rice or garlic mashed potatoes.

VARIATION:

◎ REPLACE THE MUSHROOMS WITH 1/2-INCH-THICK SLICES OF EGGPLANT.

Low-Fat Option:

◎ USE 1 TBSP OF SESAME OIL AND 1 TBSP OF OLIVE OIL OR CANOLA OIL, AND INCREASE THE LIGHT SOY SAUCE TO 3 TBSP.

Grilled Portobello Mushrooms with Penne

SERVES 4

Grilled portobello mushrooms have such a hearty, robust flavor that it reminds me of eating very tender beef. Whenever I serve this vegetarian meal, I get raves from even non-vegetarians.

2 cups	penne
2	large portobello mushrooms, stems removed
1/2 tsp	salt
1/2 tsp	black pepper
2 tbsp	butter or vegetable oil
2 cloves	garlic, minced
1 cup	button mushrooms, chopped
1/2 cup	dry red or white wine
1/2 tsp	dried basil
1/2 tsp	dried thyme
1 cup	whipping cream
1/2 cup	chopped fresh Italian parsley
1/4 cup	freshly grated Parmesan cheese

In a large pot of boiling water cook penne until tender but firm. Drain and return to pot. Meanwhile, sprinkle portobello mushrooms with salt and pepper; grill on both sides until tender and grill marks appear. In a saucepan melt the butter; sauté the garlic and button mushrooms until tender. Add the wine, basil and thyme; cook, stirring, until reduced by half. Slowly stir in the cream; allow the sauce to thicken. Stir in the parsley. Serve over drained penne. Slice the portobello mushrooms diagonally and arrange on top. Sprinkle with Parmesan cheese.

VARIATION:

- REPLACE THE GRILLED PORTOBELLO MUSHROOMS WITH GRILLED CHICKEN OR BEEF.

Low-Fat Options:

- REPLACE VEGETABLE OIL WITH VEGETABLE STOCK FOR SAUTÉING.

- REPLACE THE CREAM WITH A NON-FAT MILK BEVERAGE OR LOW-FAT SOUR CREAM. MIX WELL OVER MEDIUM HEAT SO YOU DO NOT BURN OR CURDLE THE SAUCE.

Calypso Herbed Eggplant Cutlet

SERVES 4

A native of Southeast Asia, the humble eggplant has been a staple there for four thousand years, but it took its time getting to the West. It was Thomas Jefferson, a tireless searcher for new foods, who imported the seeds, and so variety may account for the name. This Eggplant Cutlet is a wonderful vegetarian main meal. I like to serve it with rice and potatoes along with other colorful vegetables like carrots. The herbs and spices in this recipe really put a zing in it!

COATING

1/2 cup	dry bread crumbs
1 tsp	onion powder
1 tsp	garlic powder
1 tsp	paprika
1 tsp	chili powder
1/2 tsp	cayenne (optional)
1/2 tsp	dried basil
1/2 tsp	dried oregano
1/2 tsp	dried tarragon (optional)
1/2 tsp	salt
1/2 tsp	black pepper

1	medium eggplant
1	egg
1/4 cup	milk
1/4 cup	all-purpose flour
2 tbsp	vegetable oil

In a large mixing bowl combine all the coating ingredients. Slice the eggplant crosswise into 1/2-inch slices. In a shallow dish whisk together the egg and milk. Have ready in a separate dish the flour. Heat the oil in a large skillet. Dip an eggplant cutlet in flour and then into the egg mixture, and, finally, into the coating. Gently sauté the eggplant until golden, turning once. Transfer to a baking sheet and keep warm in a 250°F oven. Repeat until all of the cutlets are cooked.

Accras de Giromon et Malanga

SERVES 4

Giromon is a root vegetable similar to pumpkin, and malanga is a root vegetable similar to potato. Cook them "accras"-style, and you end up with delicious "vegetable fritters" à la St. Martin. The island is famous for its combination of French and Creole recipes. This one was created by the Mini Club in Marigot.

1/2 lb	malanga or potato
1/2 lb	giromon or pumpkin
4	garlic chives, chopped
1	green chile pepper, chopped
1 tsp	chopped fresh thyme
1 tsp	chopped fresh parsley
2 cups	all-purpose flour
1/2 tsp	salt
1/2 pkg	yeast
2	eggs, beaten
1 cup	water
2 tbsp	oil, for frying

Low-Fat Option:

◉ USE A VEGETABLE OIL LOWER IN SATURATED FAT.

Peel and grate the malangas and the giromons. In a bowl mash the malangas, giromons, garlic chives, chile pepper, thyme and parsley. In another bowl mix flour, salt, yeast, eggs and water. Mix until you get a solid pastry; add the malanga mix. In a skillet heat the oil; fry the accras, in batches, on medium heat until golden brown. Drain on paper towels and serve immediately.

◉ *Recipe from Mini Club (Marigot), St. Martin.*

Mexican Vegetables Fajitas

SERVES 2–4

The Mexican Vegetable Fajitas is a combination of vegetables and spices in a flour tortilla.

2 tbsp	vegetable oil
1	medium red onion, sliced
1	sweet red pepper, sliced
1	sweet green pepper, sliced
1	medium green or yellow zucchini, sliced lengthwise thinly
1	large carrot, shredded
2 cloves	garlic, chopped
1 tsp	chili powder
1/4 tsp	cayenne
1/2 tsp	dried basil
1/2 tsp	salt
1/2 tsp	black pepper
2	10-inch flour tortilla shells
1/2 cup	shredded tofu mozzarella

In a large skillet or sauté pan heat the oil and add the onion, peppers, zucchini, carrot and garlic. Sauté 2 minutes or until tender. Add the chili powder, cayenne, basil, salt and pepper and mix well. Sauté another 2 minutes and then remove the pan from the heat. Divide the ingredients into the two tortilla shells, fold over and sprinkle each with equal amounts of tofu cheese. Bake at 350°F until the cheese is melted, about 3–5 minutes.

VARIATIONS:

◉ USE MOZZARELLA CHEESE INSTEAD OF THE TOFU.

◉ SUBSTITUTE OTHER VEGETABLES THAT YOU HAVE AVAILABLE.

Low-Fat Options:

◉ SAUTÉ THE VEGETABLES IN 1/4 CUP LOW-SODIUM VEGETABLE STOCK INSTEAD OF OIL.

◉ USE A LIGHT TOFU MOZZARELLA.

Vegetable Chow Mein
SERVES 4

The multiplicity of the population of Jamaica is reflected in both its cuisine and the country's motto, "Out of many, one people." While most Jamaicans are of African descent, Europeans, North and South Americans and Asians are among those who have made the island their home.

6 oz	Chinese noodles or spaghetti
3 cobs	canned baby corn
3	each broccoli and cauliflower florets
2 stalks	bok choy
2	button mushrooms
1/4 lb	green beans
1/2 cup	water chestnuts
1 tbsp	vegetable oil
1 tsp	chopped garlic
1/2 tsp	chopped jalapeño peppers (optional)
2 tbsp	soy sauce
1 tsp	sesame oil
1 tbsp	cornstarch
	Salt and black pepper to taste

In a pot of boiling salted water cook the noodles until tender but firm. Drain, rinse under cold water and set aside to drain again. Meanwhile, cut baby corn, broccoli, cauliflower, bok choy, mushrooms, green beans and water chestnuts into small pieces; set aside. In a wok or large skillet heat the vegetable oil; stir-fry the noodles for 1 minute. Set aside on a serving plate. Stir-fry the garlic, corn, broccoli, cauliflower, bok choy, green beans and jalapeño pepper (if using) for 2 minutes. Stir in the water chestnuts, mushrooms, soy sauce and sesame oil. Stir-fry about 2 minutes. Stir cornstarch into 1 tbsp cold water; stir into vegetables and cook, stirring, for 1 minute. Cover the fried noodles with the cooked vegetables and serve warm.

⊚ Recipe from the Ruins Restaurant, Ocho Rios, Jamaica.

VARIATION:

⊚ ADD WHATEVER LEFTOVER VEGETABLES YOU HAVE.

Low-Fat Options:

⊚ USE A LIGHT OR LOW-IN-SATURATED-FATS VEGETABLE OIL.

⊚ REPLACE THE VEGETABLE OIL WITH 1/4 CUP OF VEGETABLE STOCK AND SAUTÉ.

Health Option:

⊚ USE LOW-SODIUM SOY SAUCE.

Spicy Tofu Balls
SERVES 6

That most versatile of legumes—the soybean—is a powerhouse of nutrition, crammed full of protein, fat, vitamins and minerals. The curd of the soybean, called tofu, is produced by a cooking/jellying/reheating/sieving process. These Spicy Tofu Balls are great with Creole Sauce and rice. I had a version of this meal in a vegetarian restaurant and thought you would enjoy my variation.

I	block of firm tofu (3/4 lb)
1/2 cup	dry bread crumbs
1/2 cup	chopped fresh parsley
2 tbsp	chopped almonds
2 tbsp	yogurt or sour cream
I tbsp	soy sauce
1/2 tsp	chili powder
2	shallots OR I small onion, chopped
I	jalapeño pepper, chopped OR 1/4 tsp cayenne
I	egg, lightly beaten
2 tbsp	olive oil
I cup	Creole Sauce (recipe on page 7)

In a mixing bowl mash the tofu. Stir in the bread crumbs, parsley, almonds, yogurt, soy sauce, chili powder, shallots, jalapeño pepper and egg; mix well. Form into 20 balls. If mixture is too dry, add a bit more yogurt or sour cream. In a large skillet heat the oil; gently brown the tofu balls about 5 minutes, turning. Serve with rice or pasta and pour the Creole Sauce over top.

VARIATIONS:

◉ REPLACE THE TOFU WITH I LB OF LEAN GROUND TURKEY.

◉ USE OTHER SAUCES FROM THIS BOOK.

Low-Fat Options:

◉ USE LOW-FAT TOFU.

◉ USE LOW-FAT OR NON-FAT YOGURT OR SOUR CREAM.

Health Option:

◉ USE LOW SODIUM SOY SAUCE.

Baked Tofu with Tarragon in Red Pepper Sauce

SERVES 4–6

Tofu makes a wonderful meal, especially when combined with fresh herbs and vegetables. If you're one of those people who thinks they don't like tofu, try this recipe—you'll quickly change your mind.

2 cloves	garlic, minced
1	medium onion, chopped
1/2	fennel bulb, chopped
1/2 cup	chopped fresh tarragon
1/4 cup	chopped fresh parsley
1/2 cup	dry white wine
2 tbsp	lemon juice
1 tsp	balsamic vinegar
1/2 tsp	black pepper
1/4 tsp	salt
1	bay leaf
3	sweet red peppers, chopped
1-1/2	blocks firm tofu, cut into 1/2-inch strips

In a shallow baking dish mix together the garlic, onion, fennel, tarragon, parsley, white wine, lemon juice, balsamic vinegar, pepper, salt and bay leaf. In a food processor purée red peppers with 3 tbsp of the marinade. Reserve 1/2 cup of the red pepper purée for garnish. Stir remaining purée into marinade. Add tofu, turning to coat well, and marinate the tofu 15 minutes, turning occasionally. Bake at 350°F for 10 minutes, turning occasionally, until tofu is firm on the outside and cooked through. Arrange tofu on plates and garnish with reserved red pepper purée.

VARIATION:

- REPLACE THE TOFU WITH LARGE PORTOBELLO MUSHROOMS AND GRILL RATHER THAN BAKE.

Low-Fat Option:

- THIS RECIPE IS PRETTY LOW IN CALORIES, BUT YOU CAN REPLACE THE WHITE WINE WITH WHITE GRAPE JUICE OR APPLE JUICE.

Tofu Stir-Fry with Spicy Tomatoes and Ginger

SERVES 4–6

A stir-fry is a quick and simple way to combine your favorite vegetables. I have made this dish a bit different by adding some ginger to give it an island flair.

1	block firm tofu, cubed
2 tsp	paprika
1/2 tsp	cayenne
1 tbsp	vegetable oil
4 cloves	garlic, minced
1 cup	shredded purple cabbage
1/2 cup	chopped fennel bulb
1/2 cup	shredded carrot
1 tsp	chopped fresh ginger
1 can	stewed tomatoes (19 oz/540 mL)
1 bunch	green onions, chopped
1/2 cup	shredded fresh basil
1 tsp	chopped jalapeño or other hot peppers
1/4 cup	soy sauce
1 tsp	balsamic vinegar

Arrange tofu cubes on a greased baking sheet. Stir together the paprika and cayenne; sprinkle over tofu. Bake tofu at 350°F for 10 minutes. Meanwhile, in a wok or large skillet heat the oil; sauté the garlic, cabbage, fennel, carrots and ginger for 2 minutes. Add the tomatoes, green onions, basil, jalapeño pepper, soy sauce, balsamic vinegar and tofu; cook for another 2–3 minutes, mixing well.

VARIATION:

- REPLACE THE TOFU WITH CUBED CHICKEN OR BEEF.

Health Option:

- USE CALORIE-REDUCED FIRM TOFU.

Vegetable and Tofu Brochettes

SERVES 6

Here's a vegetarian recipe that has it all—vegetables, spices, marinade, tofu—and skewers to grill all of these delights. Summer or winter, it's a great meal that everyone will love. You can even prepare it in advance, then grill it inside or out. And guess what? You'll never miss the meat!

2 cloves	garlic, chopped
1/2 cup	apple juice
1/2 cup	apple juice concentrate
1/2 cup	dry white wine
1 tbsp	olive oil
1 tsp	dried basil
1 tsp	dried oregano
1 tsp	dried tarragon
1/2 tsp	cinnamon
1/2 tsp	salt
1/2 tsp	black pepper
2	apples, peeled, cored and cut in chunks
1 lb	firm tofu, cut in 1-inch cubes
2	sweet peppers, cut into chunks
1	large zucchini, cubed
1 cup	sliced assorted mushrooms
4	apples, cut in wedges
1 cup	chopped fennel bulb
1	medium red onion, cut into chunks

Soak six 8-inch wooden skewers for 30 minutes. In a food processor purée the garlic, apple juice, apple juice concentrate, white wine, oil, basil, oregano, tarragon, cinnamon, salt, pepper and apple chunks. Add the tofu, peppers, zucchini, mushrooms, apple wedges and fennel; toss to coat well. Thread the onion chunks, tofu, apple wedges and vegetables onto skewers and arrange skewers in a shallow baking dish. Pour marinade over skewers and marinate for at least 1 hour. Grill until grill marks appear, about 5–8 minutes, basting with the marinade.

VARIATION:

◉ To make this a seafood dish, replace the tofu with 2 swordfish steaks, cubed.

Health Option:

◉ Use a low-calorie firm tofu.

Seafood

Lotus Lily Lobster

SERVES 4

On the edge of Ocho Rios, Jamaica, in a spectacular natural setting, sits the Ruins Restaurant. There is an abundance of flora, and terrace dining by an enchanting waterfall. The Ruins combines Jamaican and oriental food, a good example of which is Lotus Lily Lobster.

2 tbsp	vegetable oil
2 lb	lobster meat, cut into 1-1/2-inch pieces
2 cups	chicken stock
2	green onions, sliced
1 clove	garlic, minced
1	small onion, chopped
3 tbsp	dry sherry
2 tbsp	oyster sauce
1 tsp	sugar
1 tsp	chopped fresh ginger
1 tsp	sesame oil
1 tsp	soy sauce
1 tbsp	cornstarch
1 tbsp	water
	Salt and black pepper to taste

VARIATION:

⊙ REPLACE THE LOBSTER WITH 16 LARGE TIGER SHRIMP.

Health Options:

⊙ USE A LIGHT SOY SAUCE (IT'S LOWER IN SODIUM).

⊙ USE LOW-SODIUM CHICKEN STOCK.

⊙ REPLACE THE SUGAR WITH CALORIE-REDUCED LIQUID SWEETENER.

Heat the oil in a wok or large skillet; stir-fry the lobster for 2 minutes. Pour off excess oil. Add the chicken stock, green onions, garlic, onion, sherry, oyster sauce, sugar, ginger, sesame oil, soy sauce, salt and pepper to the lobster. Cook over low heat for 10 minutes. Whisk the cornstarch into the water; stir mixture into the sauce, stirring continuously until the desired consistency is reached.

Mexican Stuffed Prawns

SERVES 4

Cozumel was where I first tried this version of stuffed prawns. This dish has both a sweet and a hot taste.

16	jumbo prawns, peeled and deveined
1 8-oz can	crabmeat
1 tbsp	Dijon mustard
1 tsp	soy sauce
1 tsp	balsamic vinegar
1 tsp	liquid honey
1 tsp	chili powder
4 cloves	garlic, minced
2	oranges, halved

SAUCE

1 cup	chopped fresh coriander
1/4 cup	orange juice
1 tbsp	lime juice
1 tbsp	liquid honey
1 tsp	sesame oil
1/4 tsp	cayenne

Cut prawns along the spine, from head to tail, and butterfly to make a cavity for the stuffing. In a bowl combine crabmeat, mustard, soy sauce, balsamic vinegar, honey, chili powder and garlic. Stuff the shrimp with the mixture and skewer the prawns individually. In a small bowl combine all sauce ingredients. Brush some of the sauce on the shrimp; grill shrimp for 2–3 minutes. Place 4 shrimp, standing up, into the halved oranges, and surround with rice, peppers and red beans. Serve with remaining sauce for dipping.

VARIATION:

- REPLACE THE CRABMEAT WITH 1 CUP OF FINELY CHOPPED MUSHROOMS.

Health Options:

- REPLACE THE HONEY WITH CALORIE-REDUCED LIQUID SWEETENER.
- USE A LOW-SODIUM SOY SAUCE.

Mussels Steamed with Chili and Red Wine

SERVES 4-6

Mussels are easy to prepare and this recipe makes preparation very quick. The Mexican combination of flavors creates a different twist for mussels.

3 lbs	cleaned mussels
1	sweet red pepper, finely chopped
1 bunch	green onions, finely chopped
1/2 cup	chopped fresh parsley

SAUCE

3/4 cup	dry red wine
1 tsp	garlic powder
1 tbsp	chili powder
1/4 tsp	cayenne
2 tbsp	lemon juice
1 tsp	dried basil
1/2 tsp	salt
1/2 tsp	black pepper

In a large pasta pot combine the sauce ingredients. Bring to a boil and add the mussels, red pepper, green onions and parsley, mixing in the liquid well. Cover and simmer on low heat for 10 minutes or until mussels open. If liquid reduces, add more wine. Discard any mussels that do not open. Serve with a Mexican-style rice with black or red kidney beans.

VARIATION:

◉ REPLACE CHILI POWDER WITH SAME AMOUNT OF MILD CURRY POWDER AND REPLACE PARSLEY WITH CORIANDER. FLAVOR WILL DIFFER SLIGHTLY.

Low-Fat Option:

◉ REPLACE RED WINE WITH WATER.

◉ *Recipe from L'Arhawak (Marigot), St. Martin.*

Baked West Indian Fish
SERVES 4

This baked fish is a recipe you'll repeat using various sauces.
I have done it with the Island Orange-Prune Sauce (page 11) and with
Ken's Mexican Salsa (page 15). Try whatever appeals to your taste
buds that day.

4	plum tomatoes, chopped
2	apples, chopped
2 cloves	garlic, minced
1/2 cup	apple juice
1/4 cup	chopped fresh parsley
1/4 cup	chopped chives or green onions
1 tsp	mild curry powder or paste
1/2 tsp	salt
1/2 tsp	black pepper
1/4 tsp	cinnamon
1/4 tsp	ground cloves
4	red snapper fillets
1	bay leaf

Low-Fat Option:

⊙ REPLACE THE RED
SNAPPER WITH SOLE.

In a food processor combine the tomatoes, apples,
garlic, apple juice, parsley, 2 tbsp of the chives, curry
powder, salt, pepper, cinnamon and cloves; purée until
smooth.

Place the fillets and bay leaf in a large baking dish.
Cover with the sauce. Bake at 350°F for 8–10 minutes,
until fish has turned pink but is not flaky. Discard
bay leaf.

Island Mixed Grill with Coconut-Banana Rice

SERVES 2–4

I wait until I'm at the local supermarket to decide on what seafood to use in this recipe. If you would like to add some fruit or vegetables to the skewers for color, that would be fine.

2 cups	basmati rice
2 cups	water
1 cup	unsweetened coconut milk
1	banana, sliced
1/2 cup	raisins
1 tsp	shredded unsweetened coconut (optional)
1 tbsp	garlic powder
1 tbsp	onion powder
1 tbsp	paprika
1 tbsp	sesame seeds
1 tsp	dried basil
1 tsp	dried thyme
1/2 tsp	cayenne
1/2 tsp	salt
1/2 tsp	black pepper
1/4 tsp	dried sage
1/4 tsp	cinnamon
1/4 tsp	ground cloves
1	tuna steak
2	large salmon steaks
6	jumbo tiger shrimps or prawns
6	jumbo bay scallops
1 tbsp	lemon rind

VARIATION:

◎ REPLACE THE TUNA WITH CHICKEN OR SWORDFISH.

Low-Fat Option:

◎ REPLACE COCONUT MILK WITH APPLE JUICE.

Soak six bamboo skewers for 30 minutes. Boil basmati rice in water, coconut milk and banana 15–20 minutes; stir in raisins and coconut (if using) toward the end.

Meanwhile, in a bowl stir together garlic powder, onion powder, paprika, sesame seeds, basil, thyme, cayenne, salt, pepper, sage, cinnamon and cloves. Cut tuna and salmon into 6-inch cubes; dredge in seasoning mix and thread on skewers. Dredge shrimp in seasoning mix and thread on skewers. Repeat with scallops. Grill skewers for 2 minutes; sprinkle with half of the lemon rind. Turn and grill another 3–4 minutes, until seafood is cooked through; sprinkle with remaining lemon rind. Serve grilled seafood over rice.

island Grilled Seafood

SERVES 6

You can cook the seafood on an indoor grill, on a barbecue or under the broiler.

1/2 cup	chopped fresh tarragon
1/2 cup	orange juice
1/2 cup	light soy sauce
1/3 cup	Grand Marnier
1/2 cup	chopped fresh parsley
1/2 cup	chopped fresh mint
2 tbsp	chopped fresh thyme
1 tbsp	garlic powder
1 tbsp	onion powder
1/2 tsp	cayenne
1/2 tsp	black pepper
10	tiger shrimp, peeled
6	whole squid, cleaned and sliced
2	swordfish steaks, each cut into 4 pieces
1/2 cup	dry white wine
4 cloves	garlic, minced
2 lb	mussels, cleaned

In a bowl combine tarragon, orange juice, soy sauce, Grand Marnier, 1/4 cup of the parsley, 1/4 cup of the mint, thyme, garlic powder, onion powder, cayenne and black pepper. Set aside 1/4 cup marinade for basting. Add shrimp, squid and swordfish to marinade, turning to coat well. Marinate seafood, covered and refrigerated, at least 15 minutes and preferably overnight.

Combine white wine and garlic in foil; add mussels and place on grill with shrimp, squid and swordfish. Close grill and cook, basting occasionally with reserved marinade, until seafood is cooked through. Discard any mussels that do not open. Arrange mussels in the center of a platter and surround with seafood. Garnish with remaining parsley and mint.

VARIATION:

⊙ REPLACE SEAFOOD WITH MEAT SUCH AS PORK, BEEF, CHICKEN AND ITALIAN SAUSAGE TO MAKE A CALYPSO GRILLED MEAT PLATTER.

Low-Fat Options:

⊙ LEAVE OUT THE GRAND MARNIER.

⊙ REPLACE THE WHITE WINE WITH APPLESAUCE OR APPLE JUICE.

Calypso Crab Casserole
SERVES 4

The following casserole is quick and healthy. You can experiment by adding other seafood according to your taste. Your taste buds will jump from island to island.

1 7.5-oz can	tuna in water
1 7.5-oz can	salmon in water
1 7.5-oz can	crabmeat
1 cup	chopped celery
1	medium red onion, chopped
1	sweet red pepper, chopped
1/2 cup	chopped fresh parsley
1 cup	dry bread crumbs
2	eggs
1 tsp	garlic powder
1 tsp	paprika
1/2 cup	freshly grated Parmesan cheese
1/2 cup	shredded mozzarella cheese
1/2 tsp	salt
1/2 tsp	black pepper

In a large mixing bowl combine the tuna, salmon, crabmeat, celery, onion, red pepper, parsley, bread crumbs, eggs, garlic powder, paprika, Parmesan cheese, salt and pepper. Mix well and place in large casserole dish. If mixture is too dry, add 2 tbsp of yogurt or sour cream. Bake at 350°F for 20 minutes and then sprinkle with the mozzarella cheese. Bake another 10 minutes or until golden.

VARIATION:

⊚ REPLACE CANNED CRAB-MEAT WITH CANNED SHRIMP.

Low-Fat Option:

⊚ LEAVE OUT PARMESAN CHEESE AND REPLACE THE MOZZARELLA WITH A LOW-FAT VERSION.

Mariñated Tuña

SERVES 4

This recipe can be served as an appetizer or as part of a main course.

	Juice of half a lime
1 tbsp	mango juice
1-1/2 tsp	unsweetened coconut milk
1 tsp	chopped fresh chives
1/4 lb	thinly sliced raw tuna
1 tsp	cocoa powder

In a bowl stir together the lime juice, mango juice, coconut milk and chives. Marinate the tuna for 1–2 hours, covered and refrigerated. Sprinkle with cocoa powder. Serve chilled on toast.

© *Recipe from L'Arhawak (Marigot), St. Martin*

Poached Salmon in Pineapple

SERVES 4

Poaching is one of my favorite ways of preparing fish and poultry. A lot of people think you cannot overcook food by poaching but you can dry out fish and poultry if you are not careful.

2 cups	pineapple juice
1 cup	chopped pineapple
1/2 cup	dry white wine
2 cloves	garlic, minced
1	medium red onion, chopped
1	sweet yellow pepper, chopped
1 tbsp	balsamic vinegar
1 tsp	dried basil
1 tsp	dried tarragon
1 tsp	dried oregano
1/2 tsp	black pepper
1/4 tsp	salt
4	salmon steaks

In a large deep skillet bring to a boil the pineapple juice, pineapple, white wine, garlic, onion, yellow pepper, balsamic vinegar, basil, tarragon, oregano, pepper and salt. Reduce heat and simmer for 10 minutes; add the salmon steaks and poach until the salmon is completely opaque, about 10 minutes, turning once.

VARIATION:

- REPLACE THE SALMON WITH CHICKEN.

Low-Fat Options:

- REPLACE THE PINEAPPLE JUICE WITH WATER.
- REPLACE THE WHITE WINE WITH GRAPE OR APPLE JUICE.

Grilled Salmon with Tangy Grapefruit Sauce

SERVES 4

I like to combine seafood and grapefruit because it makes for a very tangy flavor. The herbs also add a very fresh taste to fish and sauce.

4	salmon fillets
1-1/4 cups	grapefruit juice
1	medium grapefruit, peeled and cut in small pieces (1 cup)
1 tsp	olive oil
2	green onions, chopped
1/2 cup	dry white wine
2 tbsp	chopped fresh dill
1 tsp	grapefruit rind
1/4 tsp	salt
1/2 tsp	black pepper
1/2 cup	low-fat sour cream or yogurt
1/2 cup	table or half-and-half cream
	Grapefruit slices, for garnish

In a shallow glass dish marinate salmon in 1/2 cup of grapefruit juice and a few grapefruit pieces for approximately 15 minutes, turning occasionally. In a medium saucepan over medium heat, heat the oil; sauté onions until tender. Add wine and raise heat, cooking for 3–4 minutes to reduce liquid. Add remaining grapefruit juice, 1/2 cup of the grapefruit pieces, dill, grapefruit rind, salt and pepper; simmer 10 minutes. Stir in sour cream and table cream; allow liquid to thicken, stirring constantly. Do not boil or sour cream will curdle. Keep sauce warm. Grill salmon and grapefruit slices, occasionally brushing with the remaining grapefruit juice, 3–4 minutes each side until salmon turns pink. Garnish with grapefruit slices.

VARIATIONS:

- REPLACE THE SALMON WITH OTHER SEAFOOD LIKE SWORDFISH OR TUNA.

- REPLACE THE SALMON WITH CHICKEN BREASTS.

- REPLACE THE ENTIRE GRAPEFRUIT MIXTURE WITH ORANGES TO CREATE AN ORANGE SAUCE.

Low-Fat Options:

- REPLACE THE TABLE CREAM WITH 1/2 CUP LOW-FAT SOUR CREAM.

- LEAVE OUT THE SOUR CREAM OR CREAM, ADD 2 CUPS GRAPEFRUIT JUICE AND POACH THE SALMON.

Crispy Sole with Island Herbs and Spices

SERVES 4

For lunch in the Island Café on the Century, I had a version of this delicious breaded sole. If you want to try something a little different, add 1/4 cup grated Parmesan cheese to the bread crumb mixture.

1/2 cup	dry bread crumbs
1 tsp	garlic powder
1 tsp	onion powder
1 tsp	paprika
1/2 tsp	chili powder
1/2 tsp	dried basil
1/2 tsp	dried oregano
1/2 tsp	dried thyme
1/2 tsp	salt
1/2 tsp	black pepper
1/2 tsp	mild curry powder (optional)
1/4 tsp	cayenne
2	eggs, well beaten
1/4 cup	all-purpose flour
4	large sole fillets
2 tbsp	vegetable oil
1	lemon, quartered, for garnish
	Caribbean Fruit Salsa (recipe on page 12)
	(optional)

In a shallow dish combine the bread crumbs, garlic powder, onion powder, paprika, chili powder, basil, oregano, thyme, salt, pepper, curry powder (if using) and cayenne. Have ready in two separate dishes eggs and flour. Working with one fillet at a time, dust fish with flour. Coat with egg, letting excess drip off. Roll fish in bread crumb mixture, coating thoroughly. In a large skillet heat the oil; gently fry the fish until flesh is cooked through and outside is golden brown, turning once. Garnish with lemon wedges and Caribbean Fruit Salsa (if using).

VARIATION:

◎ SUBSTITUTE RED SNAPPER OR A CHICKEN CUTLET FOR THE SOLE.

Low-Fat Option:

◎ INSTEAD OF FRYING, SPRAY A COOKIE SHEET WITH VEGETABLE COOKING SPRAY AND BAKE THE FISH AT 350°F FOR 9–12 MINUTES, UNTIL NEARLY COOKED THROUGH. BROIL FOR 3 MINUTES OR UNTIL GOLDEN BROWN.

Oven-Baked Spicy Sole

SERVES 4

Sole is one of the most common fish and can always be found fresh or frozen in your local supermarket. I had a version of this recipe in Jamaica and was determined to prepare it myself when I got home.

1 tsp	dried basil
1 tsp	dried thyme
1 tsp	cayenne
1 tsp	paprika
1 tsp	onion powder
1 tsp	garlic powder
1 tsp	salt
1 tsp	black pepper
1/2 cup	dry bread crumbs
4	large sole fillets
1/4 cup	chopped fresh parsley
1 tbsp	olive oil
1 tsp	lemon juice

In a small bowl stir together basil, thyme, cayenne, paprika, onion powder, garlic powder, salt and pepper. In a shallow dish combine bread crumbs and 1 tbsp of the seasoning mixture; set aside. Sprinkle seasoning mixture evenly over both sides of fish. Stir parsley, olive oil and lemon juice into bread crumb mixture. Dip fish in crumbs, coating thoroughly. Arrange fish in a greased or nonstick baking pan. Bake at 350°F for 10–15 minutes, turning once, until fish is white.

VARIATION:

⊚ REPLACE THE SOLE WITH RED SNAPPER FILLETS (WATCH OUT FOR SMALL BONES).

Low-Fat Option:

⊚ REPLACE THE OLIVE OIL WITH CANOLA OIL, WHICH IS LOWER IN SATURATED FATS.

Mexican Fried Sole

SERVES 4

Mexican Fried Sole is a great way to prepare sole from your local supermarket. I had a version of this recipe when I visited Mexico on my cruise. I think you, too, will enjoy this one.

4	large sole fillets
1/2 cup	lemon juice
1/2 cup	dry bread crumbs (fine)
1 tsp	garlic powder
1 tsp	onion powder
1 tbsp	chili powder
1 tbsp	flour
1/4 tsp	cayenne (optional)
1/2 tsp	dried basil
1/2 tsp	black pepper
1/2 tsp	salt
2 tbsp	unsalted butter

In a shallow dish allow the sole to soak in the lemon juice about 15 minutes in the refrigerator, turning occasionally.

Combine the bread crumbs, garlic powder, onion powder, chili powder, flour, cayenne, basil, salt and pepper. Dip the sole into the dry mixture and coat both sides well.

In a sauté pan melt 1 tbsp butter. On medium heat sauté 2 pieces of fish for about 4 minutes on each side, or until golden brown. Repeat with remaining butter and other 2 pieces of fish.

Low-Fat Option:

⊚ INSTEAD OF SAUTÉING, BAKE FISH AT 350°F IN A NONSTICK BAKING DISH FOR 10 MINUTES. BROIL FOR 2 MINUTES OR UNTIL GOLDEN.

Red Snapper with Shrimp and Crabmeat

SERVES 2–4

This dish is excellent to serve when you have company. A lot of it can be prepared in advance, so while it is cooking you can spend some quality time with your guests.

2	large whole red snapper
1 cup	crabmeat
1/2 cup	small shrimp
1/2 cup	dry bread crumbs
1/2 cup	chopped fresh coriander
1/2 cup	chopped fresh basil
1/2 cup	freshly grated Parmesan cheese
1/2 cup	low-fat sour cream
1 tbsp	Dijon mustard
	Juice of one lemon
2 cloves	garlic, minced
1	medium onion, chopped
1	egg
	Salt and black pepper to taste
1	lemon, sliced

VARIATION:

◉ REPLACE THE RED SNAPPER WITH 4 MEDIUM LAKE TROUT. A SMALLER FISH LIKE TROUT WILL TAKE LESS TIME TO COOK.

Low-Fat Option:

◉ LEAVE OUT THE PARMESAN CHEESE.

Remove the head and tail of the snapper. In a bowl stir together the crabmeat, shrimp, bread crumbs, coriander, basil, Parmesan cheese, sour cream, mustard, 2 tbsp of the lemon juice, garlic, onion, egg, salt and pepper. Stuff the fish cavity. Place fish in a baking dish lightly coated with vegetable oil. Lay lemon slices over the fish. Sprinkle the remaining lemon juice over and around the fish. Bake, uncovered, at 375°F for 20 minutes or until fish is pink and the skin starts to curl. Add more lemon juice or water if baking dish is dry.

Grilled Fillet of Marinated Red Snapper with Dill and Lemon

SERVES 6

Red snapper is an island favorite—it's full of flavor and abundant in the rich waters of the Caribbean. And what better place for me to taste this recipe than at Captain Oliver's at Oyster Pond on St. Martin, where the view was magnificent! I was so pleased with this dish I had to include it in my collection of island recipes sure to please you.

1/4 cup	olive oil
2 tbsp	sunflower oil or vegetable oil
	Juice of 3 lemons
2 tbsp	finely chopped fresh dill
1 tbsp	crushed black pepper
6	red snapper fillets, each about 6 oz
	salt

In a shallow bowl whisk together the olive oil, sunflower oil, lemon juice, dill and black pepper. Add the red snapper, turning to coat well, and marinate, covered and refrigerated, for 24 hours. Remove fish from the marinade, reserving marinade. Sprinkle with salt. Grill the fish 5 minutes on each side or until cooked through. Just before serving, pour the marinade over the fish. Serve with rice pilaf and vegetables of your choice.

VARIATION:

⊚ REPLACE THE RED SNAPPER WITH SWORDFISH, SALMON OR TUNA.

Low-Fat Option:

⊚ REPLACE OLIVE OIL WITH A VEGETABLE OIL LOWER IN SATURATED FATS.

Grilled Swordfish with Sweet Red Pepper Sauce

SERVES 2–4

You'll be glad to know you can prepare this swordfish on an indoor grill or broil it in your oven or toaster oven, because you'll want to enjoy it all year long.

2	sweet red peppers, quartered
1	small red onion, quartered
1/2 cup	chopped fresh parsley OR 1 tbsp dried
1/4 cup	apple juice
2 tbsp	dry red wine
1 tsp	brown sugar
1/2 tsp	cayenne (optional)
1/4 cup	chopped fresh tarragon OR 1 tsp dried
1 tsp	paprika
1/2 tsp	salt
1/2 tsp	black pepper
4	swordfish steaks

In a bowl with a hand blender or in a food processor, chop the red peppers and onion. Add 1/4 cup of the parsley, apple juice, red wine, sugar and cayenne (if using); blend well. Transfer sauce to a microwave-safe bowl and set aside. In a small bowl combine the tarragon, paprika, salt and pepper; sprinkle over both sides of the swordfish. Grill the swordfish 10–12 minutes, until opaque and grill marks appear. Place on warm serving plate. Microwave the sweet pepper sauce at High for 3 minutes. Pour the sauce over the swordfish and sprinkle with remaining parsley.

VARIATION:

◉ REPLACE THE SWORDFISH WITH CHICKEN, TURKEY OR TUNA STEAKS. POULTRY WILL TAKE LONGER TO COOK.

Health Option:

◉ REPLACE THE BROWN SUGAR WITH AN EQUIVALENT AMOUNT OF CALORIE-REDUCED LIQUID SWEETENER.

Roasted Grouper in Banana Leaf with Glazed Plantains

SERVES 4

Two island favorites are grouper, a fish that is revered by the Chinese, and plantains, a vegetable that looks much like a banana but must be cooked to become palatable. Together they make a dish that is unforgettable—a word that also describes my stay at the Estate St. Peter Greathouse on St. Thomas in the U.S. Virgin Islands.

1	grouper fillet, about 1-1/2 lb
1 cup	unsweetened coconut milk
1/4 cup	vegetable oil
1/2 cup	spiced dark rum
2 tbsp	banana liqueur
1 tsp	chopped fresh ginger
4 cloves	garlic, minced
1	shallot, minced
	Juice of one lime
	Salt and black pepper to taste
2	plantains
1/3 cup	liquid honey
1 tbsp	cinnamon

Remove any bones from the grouper. Cut the grouper into four portions. In a shallow bowl stir together coconut milk, oil, 1/4 cup of the rum, banana liqueur, ginger, garlic, shallot, lime juice, salt and pepper; marinate the grouper, covered and refrigerated, for 2 hours. Wash banana leaf and cut crosswise into 4 sections. Place grouper on banana leaf and fold until covered. Tie with thin strips of banana leaf and place in baking dish. Bake, uncovered, at 300°F for 10–12 minutes, until leaf begins to brown.

Meanwhile, peel plantains and slice into 1-inch pieces. In a bowl gently toss plantain with honey, remaining rum and cinnamon. Bake in a baking dish at 300°F for 10 minutes or until tender. Serve grouper with glazed plantains.

VARIATIONS:

- WRAP THE FISH IN FOIL.
- REPLACE GROUPER WITH SALMON, SWORDFISH OR RED SNAPPER.
- REPLACE PLANTAINS WITH BANANAS.

Low-Fat Option:

- REPLACE THE VEGETABLE OIL WITH A FISH OR VEGETABLE STOCK.

TIP:

- BANANA LEAVES CAN BE PURCHASED AT A SPECIALTY MARKET OR PRODUCE STORE.

Grouper Creole-Style

SERVES 6

Hot, colorful and decidedly eclectic describes Caribbean cuisine to a
T, or should I say a chili? Add to it the mix of the French, Spanish
and African culinary traditions that make up Creole, and you have
a Captain Oliver's special, Grouper Creole-Style, which I sampled
during my too-brief visit.

2 tbsp	sunflower oil
3	sweet red peppers, thinly sliced
3 cloves	garlic, chopped
2	medium red onions, chopped
1	celery stalk, chopped
1/2 tsp	fresh thyme, chopped
3 tbsp	tomato paste
2 tbsp	Creole Sauce (page 7), or Jerk Sauce (page 5)
3/4 cup	water
6	grouper fillets, each about 6 oz
	Salt to taste

In a large skillet heat 1 tbsp of the oil; sauté the peppers,
garlic, onions, celery and thyme for 5 minutes. Stir in
tomato paste, Creole sauce, water and remaining oil.
Allow to simmer, covered, for 40 minutes. Add the
grouper fillets and simmer for another 10 minutes.
Season with salt. Serve with rice pilaf.

VARIATION:

⊚ REPLACE THE GROUPER
WITH SOLE; COOK
FOR 6–8 MINUTES,
DEPENDING ON
THICKNESS.

Low-Fat Option:

⊚ SAUTÉ IN FISH OR
VEGETABLE STOCK
INSTEAD OF THE OIL.

⊚ *Recipe from Captain Oliver's Resort (Oyster Pond), St. Martin.*

Chicken

Stove-Top Coconut Chicken
SERVES 4

Today's extra-virgin olive oil has the highest-quality taste and aroma, and I use it in my Stove-Top Coconut Chicken. I first sampled this wonder in Jamaica and couldn't wait to get back to my kitchen and create my own version.

2 tbsp	olive oil
4	boneless chicken breasts
1	medium red onion, chopped
4 cloves	garlic, finely chopped
1 tbsp	curry powder
1 cup	unsweetened coconut milk
1/2 cup	chicken stock
1/2 cup	chopped fresh parsley
1 tbsp	shredded unsweetened coconut
1 tbsp	chopped fresh thyme
1 tbsp	chopped fresh oregano
1/2 tsp	salt
1/2 tsp	black pepper
1/4 tsp	cinnamon (optional)

In a large deep sauté pan or skillet heat the oil; brown the chicken on both sides, about 8 minutes. Add the onion, garlic and curry powder; sauté for another 3–4 minutes. Stir in the coconut milk, chicken stock, parsley, coconut, thyme, oregano, salt, pepper and cinnamon (if using). Simmer, covered, for 30 minutes or until the chicken is cooked through.

VARIATION:

◉ REPLACE THE CHICKEN WITH TURKEY OR SWORDFISH.

Low-Fat Option:

◉ REMOVE THE SKIN FROM THE CHICKEN.

Chicken Sautéed with Peanut Sauce

SERVES 2

If you love a nutty flavor to your chicken you will love this Caribbean recipe. Serve with rice mixed with chopped fruit such as dates or prunes.

4 cloves	garlic, minced
2	shallots OR 1 small onion, chopped
1/2 cup	unsweetened coconut milk
1/2 cup	chopped fresh parsley
1/4 cup	peanut butter
1/4 cup	light soy sauce
1 tsp	chopped fresh ginger
1 tbsp	rice wine vinegar
2	boneless chicken breasts
1/2 tsp	salt
1/2 tsp	black pepper
1 tsp	sesame oil
1 tsp	vegetable oil

In a food processor combine the garlic, shallots, coconut milk, 1/4 cup of the parsley, peanut butter, soy sauce, ginger and vinegar; purée until smooth. Season the chicken with salt and pepper. In a deep skillet heat the sesame and vegetable oils. Gently sauté chicken about 10–12 minutes turning occasionally. Add the peanut sauce and simmer the chicken for about 8–10 minutes or until chicken is cooked through. Garnish with remaining parsley.

VARIATION:

◉ REPLACE THE CHICKEN WITH TURKEY OR SEAFOOD.

Low-Fat Options:

◉ USE A LIGHT SMOOTH PEANUT BUTTER.

◉ REPLACE COCONUT MILK WITH NON-FAT MILK.

Chicken Banzai
SERVES 4

Chicken Banzai is an easy recipe to prepare—the flavor comes from marinating the chicken for days.

4   large boneless, skinless chicken breasts

LIME GINGER SOY SAUCE

2   limes
1 tbsp   minced fresh ginger
2 cups   soy sauce
1/2 cup soy oil

Combine sauce ingredients. Marinate raw chicken breasts in lime ginger soy sauce for 2–3 days. Occasionally turning, bake marinated chicken breasts in a baking dish at 300°F for 25 minutes.

VARIATIONS:

- TWO CLOVES OF CHOPPED GARLIC CAN BE ADDED.
- REPLACE CHICKEN WITH NEW YORK STEAK.

Health Option:

- USE A LOW-SODIUM SOY SAUCE OR LIGHT SOY SAUCE.

- *Recipe from L'Arhawak (Marigot), St. Martin.*

Lemon Tarragon Chicken

SERVES 4

Lemon Tarragon Chicken will be a favorite at your home and will have everyone asking for more.

	Juice of 6 lemons
2 tbsp	lemon rind
1 tbsp	brown sugar
2 tbsp	frozen lemonade concentrate, thawed
2 tbsp	chopped fresh tarragon
1 tsp	rice wine vinegar
1 tsp	soy sauce
4	large boneless, skinless chicken breasts
1/2 tsp	black pepper

Combine the lemon juice, 1 tbsp of the lemon rind, sugar, lemonade concentrate, tarragon, vinegar and soy sauce in a baking dish; add the chicken and marinate for 2 hours, turning occasionally. Bake in the same dish at 350°F for 20 minutes or until chicken is cooked through. Sprinkle with remaining lemon rind and black pepper.

VARIATIONS:

◉ REPLACE CHICKEN WITH BEEF—MARINATE AND GRILL.

◉ FOR A VEGETARIAN MEAL, REPLACE CHICKEN WITH TOFU.

Health Option:

◉ REPLACE SUGAR WITH CALORIE-REDUCED LIQUID SWEETENER.

Caribbean Chicken with Asparagus and Orange
SERVES 4

These skewers can also be served as an appetizer—just double the number of skewers and use shorter ones. I serve this dish with basmati rice cooked in orange juice and garnish the plates with orange rind.

	Juice of 1 lemon
1/2 cup	soy sauce
1/2 cup	chopped fresh coriander
2 tbsp	finely chopped garlic chives
1 tbsp	liquid honey
1 tsp	white pepper
1 tsp	crushed red pepper flakes
1 tsp	chopped fresh ginger
1 tsp	rice wine vinegar
1/2 tsp	chili powder
2	large boneless chicken breasts, cut into strips
1	orange, sliced
12	asparagus spears, cut into 2-inch pieces
1	lemon, cut into wedges

Soak bamboo skewers in water for 30 minutes. In a shallow dish whisk together the lemon juice, soy sauce, 1/4 cup of the coriander, chives, honey, pepper, red pepper flakes, ginger, rice wine vinegar and chili powder. Marinate the chicken for 15 minutes. Thread chicken, orange slices (folded in half), asparagus and lemon onto skewers. Grill for 12–15 minutes or until the chicken is no longer pink inside. Garnish with the remaining coriander.

VARIATION:

◎ REPLACE THE CHICKEN WITH JUMBO SHRIMP.

Health Option:

◎ REPLACE THE HONEY WITH A CALORIE-REDUCED LIQUID SWEETENER.

Chicken Stir-Fry with Orange and Mint

SERVES 6

This stir-fry is wonderful with flavored rice or noodles.

1 tbsp	olive oil
4	boneless chicken breasts, cut into strips
4	carrots, julienned
1 cup	broccoli florets
1 cup	cauliflower florets
1	sweet red pepper, sliced
1	sweet yellow pepper, sliced
1	sweet green pepper, sliced
1 bunch	green onions, chopped
1/2	medium fennel bulb, chopped
1/4 cup	chopped fresh mint
1/4 cup	orange juice
1 tsp	orange rind

In a wok or large skillet heat the oil; brown the chicken on all sides, about 8 minutes. Remove chicken from the pan. Stir-fry carrots, broccoli and cauliflower for about 2 minutes, until tender. Add the sweet peppers, green onions, fennel and mint; stir-fry another 2 minutes. Add orange juice and rind; stir-fry another 2 minutes or until vegetables are tender-crisp. Add the chicken and toss well.

VARIATION:

⊙ FOR A WONDERFUL VEGETARIAN MEAL, REPLACE THE CHICKEN WITH A FIRM TOFU CUT IN STRIPS.

Low-Fat Option:

⊙ REPLACE THE OLIVE OIL WITH LOW-SODIUM SOUP STOCK OR 1/4 CUP OF ORANGE JUICE.

Chicken and Pineapple Stir-Fry
SERVES 4

When I prepare this Jamaican version of a Chinese dish, I feel as though I am "wokking" on a sandy beach! This delicious recipe comes from the Ruins Restaurant in Ocho Rios, Jamaica, where it might have been ordered by such celebrity guests as Pierre Trudeau, Michael Bolton or Grace Jones.

1 tbsp	vegetable oil
2	boneless chicken breasts, cut into bite-size pieces
1	green onion, chopped
1 tbsp	finely chopped garlic
1 cup	coarsely chopped fresh pineapple
1 cup	pineapple juice
2 tbsp	oyster sauce
2 tbsp	dry sherry
1 tbsp	sugar
1 tbsp	white vinegar
2 tbsp	soy sauce
1 tsp	cornstarch
	Salt to taste

Heat the oil in a wok or large skillet. Stir-fry the chicken, green onion and garlic until chicken is lightly colored. Pour off any excess fat. Stir in the pineapple, pineapple juice, oyster sauce, sherry, sugar, vinegar and soy sauce. Reduce the heat and cook for 5 minutes. Whisk cornstarch with 1 tbsp cold water; gradually add to wok, stirring continuously until the desired consistency.

VARIATION:

⊙ REPLACE THE CHICKEN WITH BEEF OR A FIRM FISH SUCH AS SWORDFISH, CUBED.

Low-Fat Option:

⊙ REMOVE THE SKIN FROM THE CHICKEN.

Chicken with Sautéed Vegetables and Raisins

SERVES 2

Here is a great way to use up your leftover vegetables. I serve this dish with rice and bananas sprinkled with some cinnamon.

1 tsp	paprika
1 tsp	black pepper
1/2 tsp	salt
1/2 tsp	dried tarragon
1/2 tsp	dried dill
1/4 tsp	dried basil
2 tbsp	vegetable oil
1 clove	garlic, minced
2	small shallots OR 1 onion, chopped
1 cup	chopped mushrooms
1/2	sweet red pepper, cut into strips
8	asparagus stalks, chopped
8	cherry tomatoes
1	medium carrot, julienned
2	large boneless chicken breasts
	Juice and rind of 1 lemon
1/2 cup	dry white wine
1/2 cup	raisins

VARIATION:

⊙ REPLACE THE CHICKEN WITH SWORDFISH OR TUNA.

Low-Fat Options:

⊙ SAUTÉ THE VEGETABLES AND CHICKEN IN LOW-SODIUM CHICKEN STOCK.

⊙ REMOVE THE SKIN FROM THE CHICKEN.

In a small bowl stir together the paprika, pepper, salt, tarragon, dill and basil; set aside. In a large skillet heat 1 tbsp of the oil; sauté the garlic and shallots until shallots are translucent. Add mushrooms, red pepper, asparagus, tomatoes and carrot. Sauté 2 minutes; remove from pan and set aside. Heat the remaining oil in the skillet and gently sauté the chicken 8–10 minutes on each side, until no longer pink inside. Sprinkle half the herb mixture on the chicken; drizzle with the lemon juice. Transfer the chicken to warm serving plates. Add the wine and remaining herb mixture to the pan; boil, stirring to scrape up any brown bits, until wine is reduced by half. Add the raisins and cooked vegetables, stirring for 30 seconds. Arrange vegetables around chicken. Garnish with lemon rind.

Honey-Glazed Chicken with Pears
SERVES 4–6

In this mouthwatering chicken dish, I have taken some Caribbean spices and combined them with honey, mustard and pears.

2 tbsp	vegetable oil
3	chicken breasts
3	chicken legs
4	pears, quartered
1/2 cup	liquid honey
1 tbsp	maple syrup
1 tbsp	Dijon mustard
1/2 tsp	cinnamon
1/2 tsp	chopped fresh thyme
1/2 tsp	chopped fresh oregano
1/2 tsp	salt
1/2 tsp	black pepper
1/4 tsp	ground cloves
1/4 tsp	ground nutmeg

In a large skillet heat the oil; brown the chicken pieces, turning occasionally, 10–12 minutes. Transfer chicken, along with pears, to a nonstick baking dish. In a small bowl, whisk together the honey, syrup, mustard, cinnamon, thyme, oregano, salt, pepper, cloves and nutmeg; set aside 1 tbsp for basting. Brush glaze on chicken and pears. Bake, uncovered, at 350°F, basting occasionally, for 15 minutes or until chicken is no longer pink inside.

VARIATIONS:

◉ REPLACE THE PEARS WITH APPLES.

◉ REPLACE THE CHICKEN WITH SALMON STEAKS, BUT COOK ONLY FOR ABOUT 15 MINUTES OR UNTIL PINK.

Low-Fat Option:

◉ REMOVE ALL SKIN FROM THE CHICKEN.

Ruins Oriental Jerk Chicken
SERVES 4

Jerk chicken and jerk pork are available at roadside stands all over Jamaica. The special flavoring combines island spices cooked into a rich, peppery marinade over pimiento wood, but I recommend my more accessible version of jerk seasoning with an oriental flavor for the Ruins Restaurant's Jerk Chicken.

1	onion, chopped
1/4 cup	Dry Jerk Seasoning (recipe on page 4)
3 tbsp	dry sherry
2 cloves	garlic, chopped
2 tbsp	oyster sauce
1 tbsp	sugar
1 tbsp	soy sauce
1 tsp	salt
4	large chicken legs, halved into thigh and drumstick
2 tbsp	beer

In a shallow bowl combine the onion, jerk seasoning, sherry, garlic, oyster sauce, sugar, soy sauce and salt. Marinate the chicken, covered and refrigerated, for 2 hours, turning occasionally. Remove chicken from marinade and bake in a shallow baking dish at 300°F for 15 minutes or until slightly browned. Sprinkle chicken with beer and grill or broil until chicken is no longer pink inside.

VARIATION:

⊚ ADD WHATEVER LEFT-OVER VEGETABLES YOU HAVE.

Health Option:

⊚ USE LOW-SODIUM SOY SAUCE.

⊚ *Recipe from The Ruins Restaurant, Ocho Rios, Jamaica*

Kelly's Grilled Jerk Chicken with Orange Sauce

SERVES 2

The origin of the word "jerk" or "jerked" in Caribbean recipes is a bit obscure. Most authorities agree, however, that it is the English form of the eighteenth-century Spanish word **charquear** or **charqui**, derived from the Peruvian Indian Quichua tribe's word **ch'arki**, meaning to prepare meat in the manner of the Quichua. The Quichua seasoned the whole pig and danced about the fire. With this combination of chicken, jerk spices and orange sauce from Kelly's Caribbean Bar, Grill and Brewery in Key West, Florida, your taste buds will do the dancing!

2	boneless chicken breasts
2 tbsp	Dry Jerk Seasoning (recipe on page 4)
	Juice and chopped pulp of one seedless orange
1 tbsp	brown sugar
1 tbsp	orange rind

Coat the chicken on both sides with the jerk seasoning and grill for about 15 minutes or until the chicken is cooked through, occasionally turning. Meanwhile, in a saucepan over medium heat, stir together the orange juice, orange pulp and brown sugar until the sauce is thick, adding more orange juice if sauce is too thick. Just before chicken is cooked through, sprinkle with orange rind. Pour sauce over cooked chicken. Serve with Saffron Rice (recipe on page 82).

VARIATION:

- REPLACE THE CHICKEN WITH 1 BLOCK OF FIRM TOFU CUT IN HALF.

Low-Fat Option:

- REMOVE THE SKIN FROM THE CHICKEN.

Health Option:

- REPLACE THE SUGAR WITH CALORIE-REDUCED LIQUID SWEETENER.

Lotus Lilly Lobster, in Ocho Rios (page 104). *Jamie Hanson*

Overleaf: For great pizzas, including those from Pizza Rolandi's in Cozumel, see pages 68–75. *Jamie Hanson*

Mexican Border Chicken
SERVES 4–6

Mexican Border Chicken is a dinner party favorite at my house. This rich red chicken can be served with a black bean soup and a rice dish to make the evening truly authentic.

3 tbsp	vegetable oil
4	chicken breasts
4	chicken legs
1/2 tsp	salt
1/2 tsp	black pepper
3 tbsp	chili powder
4 cloves	garlic, minced
1	large red onion, chopped
1	large sweet red pepper, chopped
1	sweet green pepper, chopped
1	sweet yellow pepper, chopped
2	jalapeño peppers, chopped OR 1/2 tsp cayenne
1 cup	cooked red kidney beans
1 cup	salsa (mild to hot)
1 cup	mixed stewed and crushed tomatoes
1 cup	dry red wine
1/4 cup	brown sugar
2	bay leaves

In a large skillet heat 1 tbsp of the oil. Season chicken with salt and pepper. Fry chicken until golden brown on bottom; turn and sprinkle with chili powder. Cover skillet and continue to brown chicken. Meanwhile, in an oven-safe deep pot heat the remaining oil; sauté garlic, onion, sweet peppers and jalapeño peppers until onion is translucent. Add kidney beans, salsa, tomatoes, wine, brown sugar and bay leaves; bring to a boil. Add chicken. Bake at 350°F for 15 minutes or until chicken is cooked through. Discard bay leaves.

VARIATION:

- REPLACE CHICKEN WITH SWORDFISH OR TIGER SHRIMP.

Low-Fat Option:

- REMOVE THE SKIN FROM CHICKEN.

Health Option:

- REPLACE THE BROWN SUGAR WITH A CALORIE-REDUCED LIQUID SWEETENER.

(top) Ken and two of his favourite desserts: left, Helen's Mango Cake (page 165) and Rum Cake (page 166).

Taking time off in Key West, Florida. *Jamie Hanson*

Spicy Chicken with Fennel and Peppers

SERVES 4

I've combined some interesting herbs with fennel and tomato to give this chicken dish a truly different taste. Cayenne pepper is an option in this recipe; if you don't want that kick, leave it out.

1 can	stewed tomatoes (19 oz/540 mL)
2 cloves	garlic, minced
2	green onions, chopped
1	sweet green pepper, chopped
1	sweet red pepper, chopped
1	sweet yellow pepper, chopped
1/2 cup	chopped fennel bulb
1/2 cup	chopped fresh coriander
1/2 cup	chopped fresh parsley
1/4 cup	chopped fresh mint
1/4 cup	frozen apple juice concentrate, thawed
1 tsp	chili powder
1/2 tsp	cayenne (optional)
1/2 tsp	salt
1/2 tsp	black pepper
4	skinless chicken breasts
1 tbsp	olive oil

VARIATION:

⊚ REPLACE CHICKEN WITH PORK CHOPS.

Low-Fat Option:

⊚ SAUTÉ THE CHICKEN IN A NONSTICK PAN IN CHICKEN STOCK.

In a blender or food processor process tomatoes, garlic, green onions, sweet peppers, fennel, coriander, parsley, mint and apple juice concentrate until chunky; set aside. Sprinkle chili powder, cayenne (if using), salt and pepper on both sides of chicken. In a large skillet heat the oil; sauté the chicken 8–10 minutes or until browned, turning once. Transfer chicken to a baking dish and pour sauce over the top. Bake, uncovered, at 350°F for 10–12 minutes or until chicken turns white. Broil for 2 minutes or until top is browned.

Spicy Grilled Chicken Roll-Ups

SERVES 4

The different versions of the Chicken or Turkey Roll-Ups are very popular on **What's for Dinner?** Here's one that you can grill with a spicy flavor from the Islands.

1/2 cup	chopped fresh parsley or coriander
1/4 cup	finely chopped chives or green onions
1/4 cup	Dijon mustard
1 tsp	balsamic vinegar
1/4 tsp	cayenne
4 cloves	garlic, minced
1/2	sweet red pepper, finely chopped
	Salt and black pepper to taste
4	boneless, skinless chicken breasts, halved lengthwise and pounded flat
8 slices	Swiss cheese
8 slices	lean cooked ham
2 tbsp	olive oil

Soak eight short bamboo skewers for 30 minutes. In a bowl combine the parsley, chives, mustard, vinegar, cayenne, garlic, red pepper, salt and pepper. Spread mixture over each chicken strip. Top with Swiss cheese and cooked ham. Roll up tight and secure with skewers. Brush roll-ups with olive oil and grill 8–10 minutes, turning occasionally, until chicken has cooked through.

VARIATION:

- REPLACE THE CHICKEN WITH VEAL.

Low-Fat Option:

- REPLACE THE HAM WITH LOW-CALORIE COOKED TURKEY.

Cozumel Chicken and Sweet Red Pepper Roll-Ups
SERVES 4

When we arrived in Cozumel I had a very tasty baked chicken dinner. I decided to change the recipe a bit, and this is what I came up with.

2	sweet red peppers, cut into strips
2 cloves	garlic, minced
1/2 cup	chopped fresh parsley
1/4 cup	Dijon mustard
1/4 cup	low-fat sour cream
1 tsp	chili powder
	Juice of 1 lemon
1/2 tsp	salt
1 tsp	black pepper
4	boneless, skinless chicken breasts
4 slices	Swiss cheese, halved

Finely chop half a red pepper; set aside. In a bowl whisk together the garlic, parsley, mustard, sour cream, chili powder, 1 tsp of the lemon juice, salt and 1/2 tsp of the black pepper; stir in the red pepper strips. Gently pound the chicken breasts flat between two sheets of plastic wrap. Spread the sauce over the chicken. Top each chicken breast with half a slice of Swiss cheese. Roll up the chicken and secure with a toothpick. Arrange in a nonstick baking dish and top each roll-up with half a slice of Swiss cheese. Bake at 375°F for 20 minutes or until the chicken is no longer pink inside. Sprinkle with reserved red pepper and remaining lemon juice and black pepper. Slice the roll-ups prior to serving.

VARIATION:

◎ YOU CAN CHANGE THE FLAVOR A BIT BY REPLACING THE CHICKEN WITH THINLY SLICED VEAL.

Low-Fat Options:

◎ REPLACE THE CHICKEN WITH TURKEY.

◎ LEAVE OUT THE SWISS CHEESE OR USE A CHEESE LOWER IN CALORIES.

Turkey in Curry Sauce with Chick-Peas and Rice

SERVES 4–6

I am often asked how to prepare turkey in different ways. In this recipe I have taken some West Indies ideas with curry, coconut and chickpeas.

1 cup	basmati rice
2 cups	orange juice
2	boneless turkey breasts
1 tbsp	vegetable oil
2 cloves	garlic, minced
1/2 cup	unsweetened coconut milk
2 tbsp	mild curry paste OR 1 tbsp mild curry powder
1 cup	cooked chick-peas
6	green onions, chopped
1	sweet green pepper, chopped
1	chile pepper, chopped
	Juice of half a lemon

Cook the basmati rice in the orange juice instead of water. Meanwhile, cut turkey into thin strips. In a large skillet or wok heat the oil. Brown the turkey with the garlic, stirring, about 8 minutes. Add coconut milk 1 tbsp at a time, stirring after each addition until blended. Stir in curry paste, chick-peas, onions, sweet pepper and chile pepper; reduce heat to low and simmer, stirring occasionally, for 15 minutes. Stir in lemon juice; simmer for 1 minute. Serve over the rice.

VARIATION:

◎ REPLACE THE TURKEY WITH CHICKEN OR BEEF.

Low-Fat Options:

◎ REPLACE THE COCONUT MILK WITH NON-FAT SOUR CREAM OR NON-FAT MILK.

◎ BROWN THE TURKEY IN LOW-SODIUM SOUP STOCK.

Ground Turkey with Curry and Raisins

SERVES 4

Spices are the dried, intensely aromatic parts of certain plants, usually the seeds, pods, berries, roots, stems, buds, bark or even sap. Originating often in faraway places, they have been the cause of dangerous voyages, exploration, wars and empire-building. The curry in this recipe, for example, is a blend of spices from India, but when we switch the peas for kidney beans, **olé!**—we're in Mexico. Serve with egg noodles.

2 tbsp	olive oil
1 lb	lean ground turkey
4	small carrots, sliced
4 cloves	garlic, finely chopped
1 can	stewed tomatoes (19 oz/540 mL)
1/2 cup	raisins
1/4 cup	chopped green onions or chives
1 tbsp	mild curry powder OR 1 tsp curry paste
1/2 tsp	chopped fresh ginger
1/2 tsp	dried oregano
1/2 tsp	salt
1/2 tsp	black pepper
1/2 cup	frozen peas

In a deep sauté pan or skillet heat the oil; brown the turkey, carrots and garlic. Drain the excess oil, if desired. Add tomatoes, raisins, green onions, curry powder, ginger, oregano, salt and pepper; simmer, stirring occasionally, for 10 minutes to allow all the flavors to combine. Stir in the peas 5 minutes before serving.

VARIATION:

⊚ REPLACE THE GROUND TURKEY WITH GROUND BEEF.

Low-Fat Options:

⊚ DRAIN ALL OF THE OIL AFTER BROWNING THE TURKEY.

⊚ REPLACE THE OLIVE OIL WITH A VEGETABLE OIL SUCH AS CANOLA, WHICH IS LOWER IN SATURATED FATS.

Meat

Spinach Wrapped in Veal and Lemon
SERVES 4–6

This is a recipe that can be used as an appetizer or main course. Your guests will love this combination of flavors with veal—even if they don't like spinach!

2 tbsp	olive oil
2 cups	chopped spinach
2 cloves	garlic
1 tbsp	chopped fresh basil
1/2	sweet red pepper, chopped
1/4 cup	lemon juice
	Salt and black pepper to taste
6	thin veal cutlets
1/2 cup	dry white wine
1	lemon, cut into 6 slices

In a saucepan using 1 tbsp of the olive oil, sauté the spinach, garlic, basil, red pepper, 1/2 the lemon juice, salt and pepper. Sauté about 5 minutes or until spinach wilts, stirring occasionally. Remove from heat and allow to cool before dividing the mixture into six and wrapping in the veal. Secure with toothpick. Heat remaining olive oil in sauté pan and add the veal. Sauté, turning occasionally, about 3 minutes or until meat starts to turn white. Add the remaining lemon juice and white wine. Place lemon slices on top of veal. Simmer another 4 minutes or until the wine has reduced by half and the meat is cooked.

VARIATIONS:

◎ REPLACE VEAL WITH CHICKEN.

◎ FOR VEGETARIANS, REPLACE VEAL WITH 1/4-INCH OF EGGPLANT.

Low-Fat Option:

◎ SAUTÉ IN VEGETABLE STOCK RATHER THAN OLIVE OIL.

Calypso Beef Casserole
SERVES 4–6

I can honestly say that whenever I prepare this dish I get a lot of compliments. This is also a good dish to freeze and just pop right in the oven. If you want to change the flavor slightly, replace the curry with 1 tbsp of chili powder and add some canned red kidney beans.

1 tbsp	paprika
1 tsp	dried basil
1 tsp	dried tarragon
1 tsp	dried mint
1 tsp	mild curry powder
1 tsp	salt
1 tsp	black pepper
1/2 tsp	cayenne
1/2 tsp	cumin
1 lb	flank steak, cubed
4 cloves	garlic, minced
1	medium red onion, chopped
2	carrots, sliced
1/2 cup	beef stock
2–3	potatoes, thinly sliced to make a crust
1 cup	broccoli florets
1 cup	cauliflower florets
1 cup	chopped purple cabbage
1/4 cup	freshly grated Parmesan cheese
1/2 cup	shredded mozzarella cheese

VARIATION:

⊙ THIS IS A GOOD RECIPE FOR EXPERIMENTING WITH FLAVORS. REPLACE SOME OF THE DRIED HERBS WITH OTHERS SUCH AS THYME, OREGANO OR DRY MUSTARD.

Low-Fat Options:

⊙ REPLACE THE BEEF WITH A LARGE SWORDFISH STEAK AND IT WILL BECOME CALYPSO SEAFOOD CASSEROLE. YOU WON'T HAVE TO SAUTÉ THE SWORDFISH; IT WILL BAKE PRETTY QUICKLY.

⊙ USE LOW-FAT CHEESES.

In a small bowl stir together the paprika, basil, tarragon, mint, curry powder, salt, pepper, cayenne and cumin. Toss steak cubes with half the spice mixture to coat well. In a large sauté pan or skillet, brown the steak. Remove from heat. Sauté the garlic and onion in a wok or skillet, until the onions are translucent. Add the carrots in the beef stock; gently cook for another 2 minutes. Combine the beef and vegetables. Line a large casserole dish with the potatoes, slightly overlapping them. Spoon the beef mixture into the casserole dish with the broccoli, cauliflower and cabbage. Sprinkle with the remaining spice mixture, Parmesan cheese and mozzarella cheese. Bake, uncovered, at 350°F for 10 minutes or until the vegetables are cooked and cheese is brown and starting to bubble.

Island Beef Brochettes with Coconut Milk and Honey

SERVES 6–8

Skewering meat to cook it over an open flame has been around since the discovery of fire itself. In tribal times, the whole animal was roasted on a spit for communal meals, but with the evolution of the family unit smaller portions were interspersed with vegetables and other delicacies to make more convenient-sized meals. Whether it's called kebab, **en brochette** or just plain skewered, it's a bite-size treat. Using my marinade enhances the flavor even more!

1/2 cup	unsweetened coconut milk
1/4 cup	chopped fresh coriander (optional)
1/4 cup	liquid honey
1/4 cup	light soy sauce
1/2 tsp	black pepper
4 cloves	garlic
1-1/2 lb	top round, cut into 1/2-inch slices
12–16	cherry tomatoes
1 tbsp	unsweetened coconut flakes, for garnish

Soak six or eight wooden skewers for 30 minutes. In a food processor purée the coconut milk, coriander (if using), honey, soy sauce, pepper and garlic. Set aside 2 tbsp of the marinade for basting. Transfer remaining marinade to a shallow baking dish. Skewer the beef and cherry tomatoes alternately—2 tomatoes per skewer. Marinate skewers at least 20 minutes, covered and refrigerated, turning occasionally. Grill the brochettes 5–7 minutes, basting occasionally with the reserved marinade. You will know they are cooked by the grill marks on the beef and tomatoes. Sprinkle with coconut and serve immediately.

VARIATIONS:

◎ USE CUBED LEAN PORK INSTEAD OF BEEF.

◎ USE CUBED SWORDFISH INSTEAD OF BEEF.

Low-Fat Option:

◎ USE CUBED TURKEY INSTEAD OF BEEF.

Health Option:

◎ REPLACE THE HONEY WITH A CALORIE-REDUCED LIQUID SWEETENER.

Fajitas Especiales
SERVES 4–6

Pancho's Backyard Restaurant in Cozumel, Mexico, is on the main street of the town and has a regular Mexican clientele as well as tourists. People come from miles around for this very special beef fajitas dish. It must be the Corona beer!

3/4 cup	Corona beer
Pinch	garlic salt
Pinch	salt
Pinch	pepper
1	beef tenderloin, about 1/2 lb, cut into strips
1 tbsp	corn oil
1/2	sweet green pepper, julienned
1/4	white onion, julienned
1	plum tomato, julienned
6	flour tortillas

In a shallow bowl stir together the beer, garlic salt, salt and pepper; marinate the beef at least 5 minutes. In a skillet sauté the marinated beef in the corn oil. After 8 minutes, stir in the green peppers and onion. When beef is almost done, stir in the tomato. Serve on warm flour tortillas with guacamole and refried beans.

VARIATION:

⊘ FOR A VEGETARIAN MEAL REPLACE THE BEEF WITH 2 CUPS OF SLICED ASSORTED MUSHROOMS (BUTTON, PORTOBELLO AND SHIITAKE).

Low-Fat Option:

⊘ REPLACE THE BEEF WITH CHICKEN OR TURKEY.

Ginger Mixed Grill
SERVES 6-8

Serve this dish when you know your company all have different tastes. This way something will be served to accommodate everyone.

2 lb	sirloin steak, cut into 6 portions
4	lamb chops
2	chicken breasts
2	chicken legs

MARINADE

3/4 cup	light soy sauce
1/2 cup	chopped fresh parsley
1/2 cup	chopped fresh coriander
1/2 cup	dry white wine
1 tbsp	chopped fresh rosemary
1 tbsp	chopped fresh ginger
1 tbsp	Dijon mustard
1 tbsp	liquid honey
1 tsp	black pepper
1 tsp	Worcestershire sauce
2 cloves	garlic, minced
	Salt to taste

In a blender or mixing bowl blend or whisk together all the marinade ingredients. Set aside 1/4 cup of marinade for basting. In a large shallow baking dish pour marinade over the meat and chicken. Cover and refrigerate for at least 15 minutes (the longer the better). Grill, basting occasionally, until meat is cooked and chicken is no longer pink.

VARIATION:

◉ REPLACE THE MEAT WITH A SELECTION OF FISH OR OTHER MEATS.

Health Option:

◉ REPLACE THE HONEY WITH A CALORIE-REDUCED LIQUID SWEETENER.

Mexican Chili Pasta

SERVES 6

When I was growing up, I always enjoyed chili poured over pasta. This is one of my "comfort food" recipes.

1 tbsp	vegetable or olive oil
1 lb	lean ground beef
4 cloves	garlic, minced
3	celery stalks, chopped
2	sweet green peppers, chopped
1	medium onion, chopped
1/2 cup	dry red wine
1 can	stewed tomatoes (19 oz/540 mL)
1/2 cup	shaved carrots
1/2 cup	cooked kidney beans
2 tbsp	chili powder
2 tbsp	Dijon mustard
1/2 tsp	cayenne
1/2 tsp	dried basil
1/2 tsp	dried thyme
1/2 tsp	salt
1/2 tsp	black pepper
2	bay leaves

In a large sauté pan or skillet heat 1-1/2 tsp of the oil; sauté the ground beef about 5 minutes. With a slotted spoon, transfer the beef to a bowl. In the pan add the remaining oil and sauté the garlic, celery, green pepper and onion, stirring, until onion is translucent. Add the beef and wine; simmer, stirring occasionally, until wine has reduced by half. Add tomatoes, carrots, kidney beans, chili powder, mustard, cayenne, basil, thyme, salt, pepper and bay leaves; simmer, stirring occasionally, for 15 minutes. Discard bay leaves. Serve over spaghetti.

VARIATION:

◉ REPLACE THE RED WINE WITH 3/4 CUP OF BEER. IT REALLY GIVES THE CHILI A DIFFERENT FLAVOR.

Low-Fat Options:

◉ USE LEAN GROUND TURKEY INSTEAD OF BEEF.

◉ USE VEGETABLE OR BEEF STOCK FOR SAUTÉING RATHER THAN OIL.

Yucatan Beef Stew

SERVES 6

A hearty beef stew tastes great on those cold winter nights. This Mexican version makes it even more interesting with the addition of the beans, chili powder and cayenne pepper.

2 tbsp	olive oil
2 lb	lean stewing beef
2 cloves	garlic, minced
2	potatoes, cubed
2	carrots, cubed
2	celery stalks, chopped
1	medium onion, chopped
1	zucchini, cubed
1	sweet green pepper, chopped
1 can	stewed tomatoes (28 oz/796 mL)
1 cup	sun-dried tomatoes, chopped
1/2 cup	chopped fresh basil
1/2 cup	cooked red kidney beans
1/2 cup	dry red wine
1 tbsp	chopped fresh oregano
1 tbsp	chopped fresh rosemary
1 tbsp	Worcestershire sauce
1 tsp	chili powder
1/2 tsp	cayenne
2	bay leaves
1 cup	beef stock
	Salt and black pepper to taste

VARIATION:

⊘ USE WHATEVER VEGETABLES YOU HAVE ON HAND. YOU CAN ALSO USE DIFFERENT TYPES OF BEANS.

Low-Fat Option:

⊘ REPLACE THE STEWING BEEF WITH CUBED TURKEY BREAST.

In a large pot heat 1 tbsp of the oil; sauté the beef, turning occasionally, until brown. With a slotted spoon, transfer beef to a bowl. Add remaining oil to the pot; sauté the garlic, potatoes, carrots, celery, onion, zucchini and green pepper until vegetables are tender but not overdone. Add stewed tomatoes, sun-dried tomatoes, basil, kidney beans, red wine, oregano, rosemary, Worcestershire sauce, chili powder, cayenne and bay leaves. Bring to a boil, reduce heat and simmer, covered, stirring occasionally. Add beef stock, beef, salt and pepper; cover and simmer another 20 minutes. Discard bay leaves.

Peanut Beef Satay with Tomatoes

SERVES 6

I occasionally serve this recipe as an appetizer, but here I have done it as a main course. Pair it with rice cooked in pineapple juice to complete the Caribbean theme.

4 cloves	garlic, minced
2	small shallots, chopped
1/4 cup	chopped fresh basil
1/4 cup	chopped fresh coriander
1/4 cup	soy sauce
2 tbsp	unsalted peanuts
1/2 tsp	cayenne
1/2 tsp	brown sugar
1/2 tsp	salt
3 tbsp	vegetable oil
2 lb	sirloin steak, cut into 1- x 2-inch cubes
1	fennel bulb, sliced
20	cherry tomatoes

Soak eight 8-inch wooden skewers for 30 minutes. In a food processor combine garlic, shallots, basil, coriander, soy sauce, peanuts, cayenne, brown sugar and salt; purée until smooth. In a saucepan heat the marinade with oil for 8 minutes. Set aside 1/2 cup of marinade for basting. In a shallow bowl toss the steak with the marinade. Thread meat, fennel and tomatoes onto the skewers. Grill to perfection, basting occasionally with reserved marinade.

VARIATION:

⊙ USE CUBED FIRM TOFU INSTEAD OF BEEF. THE GRILLING TIME WILL BE SHORTER.

Low-Fat Option:

⊙ REPLACE THE BEEF WITH TURKEY OR SWORDFISH.

Cajun Salisbury Steak with Sweet Onion Relish

SERVES 4

Serve this dish with potatoes mashed with some garlic and dill and you will be very popular at your house.

1-1/2 lb	lean ground beef or pork
1	sweet red pepper, finely chopped
1	sweet green pepper, finely chopped
1/2 cup	dry bread crumbs
1/4 cup	Dijon mustard
1 tsp	chili powder
1/2 tsp	chopped jalapeño peppers
1/2 tsp	onion powder
1/2 tsp	garlic powder
1/2 tsp	paprika
1/2 tsp	black pepper
1/2 tsp	dried basil
1/4 tsp	dried thyme
1	egg, lightly beaten
2 tbsp	vegetable oil
4	red onions, chopped
1/4 cup	apple juice
1 tbsp	brown sugar

VARIATION:

○ SUBSTITUTE RED OR WHITE WINE FOR THE APPLE JUICE.

Low-Fat Option:

○ REPLACE THE GROUND BEEF OR PORK WITH GROUND TURKEY OR CHICKEN.

In a large mixing bowl stir together well the ground beef, sweet peppers, bread crumbs, mustard, chili powder, jalapeño pepper, onion powder, garlic powder, paprika, black pepper, basil, thyme and egg. Make four patties. In a skillet heat 1 tbsp of the oil; sauté Salisbury steaks, without burning, about 5 minutes on each side, until golden brown. Remove from pan and keep warm in the oven. In the skillet heat the remaining oil; sauté the red onions 3 minutes. Add the apple juice and brown sugar; sauté until onions are golden brown. Serve onion relish over the Salisbury steaks.

New York Pepper Steak
SERVES 2

"Qué puerto rico!" said Juan Ponce de León on entering San Juan Bay around 1500. And, indeed, what a rich port it is, today enjoying the highest standard of living in the Caribbean. In 1917, the people of Puerto Rico were made citizens of the United States, and in 1952, President Truman elevated the island to the status of a free commonwealth of the U.S. Small wonder, then, that American influence is so prominent, as in this recipe for New York Pepper Steak from the Chart House Restaurant.

1/2 cup	cracked black pepper
2	New York steaks, 6 oz each
1/2 tsp	salt
1	large onion
2 tbsp	butter
2 tbsp	brandy
1/4 cup	chopped fresh parsley

Press the pepper into both sides of the steaks; refrigerate, covered, for 24 hours. Remove any excess pepper from the steak, sprinkle both sides lightly with salt, and grill or broil the steak to the desired doneness. Meanwhile, cut onion into 1/4-inch slices. Heat butter and brandy in a small skillet; sauté the onion 8 minutes or until tender. Stir in the parsley. Serve the onion sauce with the grilled steak.

VARIATION:

⊘ USE OTHER CUTS OF STEAK OR BEEF.

Low-Fat Option:

⊘ USE CALORIE-REDUCED BUTTER.

⊘ *Recipe from Chart House, San Juan, Puerto Rico.*

Hot Sausage with Kidney Beans in Tomato Sauce

SERVES 4

Purchase a fairly spicy sausage that is vegetarian, beef, chicken or turkey. This common Mexican dish is almost like a stew.

1 tbsp	olive oil
3	hot sausages
4	shallots OR 1 medium red onion, chopped
1	sweet red pepper, chopped
2 cloves	garlic, minced
6	medium tomatoes, chopped
1 cup	dry red wine
1/4 cup	chopped fresh basil
1/4 cup	chopped fresh sage
1 tsp	black pepper
1/2 tsp	salt
1/2 tsp	cayenne
1	bay leaf
1 cup	cooked kidney beans

In a large sauté pan or skillet heat the oil; brown the sausages, about 4 minutes each side. Remove sausages and add shallots, red pepper and garlic; sauté, stirring, until shallots are translucent. Stir in tomatoes, red wine, basil, sage, black pepper, salt, cayenne and bay leaf; simmer. Meanwhile, slice sausages into 1-inch pieces. Add to pan with kidney beans and simmer, stirring, until sausages and beans are heated through, about 5 minutes. Discard bay leaf.

VARIATION:

○ THIS IS AN EASY DISH TO PREPARE IF YOU HAVE SOME LEFTOVERS OF KEN'S MEXICAN SALSA. ALL YOU HAVE TO DO IS ADD SOME RED WINE AND STEWED TOMATOES.

Low-Fat Option:

○ PARBOIL THE SAUSAGE: PRICK HOLES IN IT WITH A FORK AND POACH IT TO REMOVE SOME OF THE FAT.

Burgundy Pork Stew
SERVES 6–8

Sherry is a wine fortified with a dose of brandy. Its sweet, remarkably full flavor adds a richness to any soup, casserole or stew, and this Burgundy Pork Stew is no exception. I've used traditional island herbs and spices to create this recipe, a version of one I first tasted on St. Thomas in the U.S. Virgin Islands.

2 tbsp	flour
2 lb	lean stewing pork, cubed
2 tbsp	olive oil
4 cloves	garlic, chopped
3	medium potatoes, chopped
2	large carrots, diced
2	celery stalks, chopped
1	zucchini, diced
1	red onion, chopped
2 cups	beef stock
1 cup	dry red wine
1 tbsp	dry sherry
1/4 cup	chopped fresh basil
1 tbsp	chopped fresh rosemary
1 tbsp	chopped fresh thyme
1/4 tsp	cinnamon
	Salt and black pepper to taste
1	bay leaf
1	yellow onion
3	whole cloves
1/2 cup	frozen corn
1/2 cup	frozen peas
2	large tomatoes, chopped

VARIATION:

⊚ REPLACE THE STEWING PORK WITH STEWING BEEF.

Low-Fat Options:

⊚ REPLACE THE STEWING PORK WITH TURKEY.

⊚ REPLACE THE RED WINE WITH WATER OR MORE BEEF STOCK.

Flour cubed pork. In a large saucepan heat 1 tbsp of the oil; sauté the pork until brown. Using a slotted spoon, remove pork from the pan. In the fat, sauté the garlic, potatoes, carrots, celery, zucchini and red onion for 5 minutes. Add beef stock, wine, sherry, basil, rosemary, thyme, cinnamon, salt and pepper. Place the bay leaf on the yellow onion and secure it with the cloves; add to the stew and simmer for 15 minutes. Add the corn, peas and tomatoes and simmer for another 5 minutes. Discard the yellow onion.

Lemon-Dill Pork Chops with Creole Sauce

SERVES 4

Preparing pork chops on an indoor grill or outdoor barbecue is easiest, but you can also prepare these pork chops under the broiler.

1/2 cup	lemon juice
1/2 cup	soy sauce
1/4 cup	chopped fresh dill
1/4 cup	chopped fresh mint
1/4 cup	chopped fresh chives or green onions
2 tbsp	vegetable oil
1 tbsp	lemon rind
1 tbsp	liquid honey
1/2 tsp	chopped fresh ginger
1/2 tsp	black pepper
4 cloves	garlic, minced
4	pork chops
2 tbsp	Creole Sauce (recipe on page 7) (optional)

In a large baking dish whisk together lemon juice, soy sauce, dill, mint, chives, oil, lemon rind, honey, ginger, pepper and garlic. Set aside 1/4 cup of marinade for basting. Place pork chops in marinade, turning to coat well, and marinate, covered and refrigerated, at least 15 minutes and preferably overnight. Stir the Creole Sauce (if using) into the reserved marinade. Grill or broil the pork chops, basting occasionally, until meat has turned white.

VARIATION:

- REPLACE THE CREOLE SAUCE WITH JERK SAUCE (RECIPE ON PAGE 5), BUT USE HALF THE AMOUNT.

Low-Fat Options:

- TRIM THE FAT OFF THE PORK CHOPS.
- REPLACE THE PORK CHOPS WITH CHICKEN OR TURKEY.

Simmered Pork Chops in Tomatoes with Island-Fresh Herbs and Pineapple

SERVES 4

Pork is a wonderful white meat, and when combined with pineapple and tomatoes, it is very flavorful. This recipe is sure to become a regular in your household.

2 tbsp	vegetable oil
4	large pork chops
1	large red onion, chopped
2 cloves	garlic, minced
4	carrots, halved lengthwise and sliced
1 can	stewed tomatoes (28 oz/796 mL) OR 6 plum tomatoes, chopped, with 2 cups water and 1 tsp tomato paste
1 cup	fresh or canned chopped pineapple
1/2 cup	chopped fresh parsley
1/2 cup	dry red wine (optional)
2 tbsp	chopped fresh thyme
2 tbsp	chopped fresh oregano
1/2 tsp	salt
1/2 tsp	black pepper
1	bay leaf

In a deep sauté pan or skillet heat the oil; brown the pork chops on both sides, until nearly cooked through, 8–10 minutes. Remove from pan. Sauté the onion and garlic, stirring, until onion is translucent, being careful not to burn them. Add carrots and sauté another 2 minutes. Stir in tomatoes, pineapple, parsley, red wine, thyme, oregano, salt, pepper and bay leaf. Add the pork chops, cover and simmer 10 minutes or until meat has turned white. Discard bay leaf.

VARIATION:

- REPLACE ANY OF THE FRESH HERBS WITH 1/2 TSP OF DRIED. TRY OTHER SPICES, SUCH AS BASIL, ROSEMARY OR TARRAGON.

Low-Fat Options:

- TRIM THE FAT OFF THE PORK CHOPS.
- REPLACE THE PORK CHOPS WITH SKINLESS, BONELESS CHICKEN BREASTS.

Spicy Pork Brochettes with Coconut and Honey

SERVES 6

Talk about a quick recipe to prepare! This should take only about 10 minutes' preparation time, and you can marinate the pork overnight, or in the morning before you go to work. If you want some extra zing, add 1/2 tsp cayenne pepper.

1/2 cup	unsweetened coconut milk
1/4 cup	chopped fresh parsley
1/4 cup	light soy sauce
1/4 cup	liquid honey
1 tsp	chopped fresh ginger
1/2 tsp	black pepper
4 cloves	garlic, minced
1-1/2 lb	lean pork, cut into 1/2-inch slices
12	cherry tomatoes

Soak six wooden skewers for 30 minutes. In a food processor purée coconut milk, parsley, soy sauce, honey, ginger, pepper and garlic. Pour marinade into a shallow baking dish. Thread the pork and cherry tomatoes onto skewers, using 2 tomatoes per skewer. Marinate brochettes, covered and refrigerated, at least 15 minutes (longer is always better). Grill brochettes 12–15 minutes, until cooked thoroughly and there are grill marks on the pork and tomatoes.

VARIATION:

⊙ To make a vegetarian meal, use 1-1/2 lb of firm tofu instead of the pork, and add some more vegetables.

Low-Fat Option:

⊙ Replace the pork with chicken or turkey.

Spicy Caribbean Lamb Chops

SERVES 2-3

Lamb is one of my favorite meats, and my neighbor Gill and I often experiment with different ideas. This is a wonderful Caribbean version that is easy to do and you can prepare it in advance.
The lamb can be done on the grill or in the broiler. I have even pan fried the chops in a nonstick skillet and seared in the flavors. You decide.

6	thick lamb chops

SEASONING

1 tsp	paprika
1 tsp	onion powder
1 tsp	garlic powder
1 tsp	dried thyme
1 tsp	dried rosemary
1 tsp	dried basil
1 tsp	white pepper
1/2 tsp	black pepper
1/2 tsp	salt
1/2 tsp	cayenne
1/2 tsp	cinnamon
1/4 tsp	ground nutmeg

SAUCE

1 tsp	olive oil
4	sweet red peppers, chopped
2	apples or mangoes, chopped
1	small onion, chopped
1/4 cup	apple juice or mango juice
1/4 cup	frozen apple juice concentrate, thawed
1 tbsp	liquid honey

VARIATION:

◎ REPLACE THE APPLES OR MANGOES WITH OTHER FRUIT, SUCH AS PAPAYA, KIWIFRUIT OR PINEAPPLE.

Low-Fat Option:

◎ REPLACE THE LAMB WITH SKINLESS CHICKEN OR A FIRM FISH SUCH AS SWORDFISH.

SEASONING

In a bowl combine all seasoning ingredients. Spread dry mixture on a sheet of waxed paper. Coat both sides of the lamb chops. Refrigerate chops, covered, at least 15 minutes.

SAUCE

In a large skillet heat oil; sauté red peppers, apples and onion 2–3 minutes or until tender. Add apple juice, apple juice concentrate and honey; simmer until liquid has reduced by half.

Grill lamb to perfection: 5–6 minutes for rare, and 7–8 minutes for medium. Spoon sauce over the lamb chops.

Jerk Lamb Rack with Roasted Garlic and Guava Glaze

SERVES 4

Compass Point in Nassau is one of the most relaxing resorts we visited. The rooms are pastel and villas are built on stilts. This recipe was one of my favorites on the menu.

4 cloves	garlic, unpeeled
1/2 cup	guava jelly
	Rice or white wine vinegar
2	French-style racks of lamb, cleaned
1 tbsp	Dry Jerk Seasoning (recipe on page 4)
2 cloves	garlic, minced
	Salt and crushed black pepper to taste
1 tbsp	vegetable oil

To make the glaze, roast 4 cloves garlic at 350°F for 20 minutes or until soft. Squeeze garlic out of its skin and mince. In a small saucepan heat the guava jelly and the garlic. Thin the glaze with a little rice vinegar. Keep warm.

Season the lamb with Jerk Seasoning, 2 cloves minced garlic, salt and pepper. In a large oven-safe skillet or roasting pan heat the oil; sear the lamb for 1 minute on each side. Transfer lamb to the oven and roast at 350°F for 10 minutes. Slice the lamb and garnish with the glaze. Serve lamb with mashed pumpkin and seasonal vegetables.

VARIATION:

⊚ REPLACE THE RACK OF LAMB WITH 4 LARGE LAMB CHOPS OR 8 SMALLER ONES.

Low-Fat Option:

⊚ REPLACE THE LAMB WITH 4 BONELESS CHICKEN BREASTS.

⊚ *Recipe from Compass Point Beach Club, Nassau, Bahamas.*

Curry Lamb and Vegetables
SERVES 4-6

I love the rich flavor of lamb, especially when it's combined with a spice like curry.

1 tbsp	vegetable oil
1-1/2 lb	lamb, cubed
1	large red onion, chopped
4	large carrots, cubed
2	medium potatoes, cubed
1 tbsp	mild curry powder
1/2 tsp	black pepper
1/2 tsp	cinnamon
4 cloves	garlic, minced
1	sweet potato, cubed
1	large zucchini, cubed
1/2 cup	chopped fresh coriander
1/2 cup	chopped fresh parsley
1-1/2 cups	chicken stock
1 tbsp	soy sauce
1	bay leaf
1	medium yellow onion
3	whole cloves

In a large skillet heat the oil; brown the lamb on all sides. With a slotted spoon transfer the lamb to a bowl. In the oil sauté the red onion, carrots and potatoes. Stir in the curry powder, pepper, cinnamon, garlic, sweet potato, zucchini, coriander, parsley, chicken stock and soy sauce. Place the bay leaf on the yellow onion and secure it with the cloves. Add to the skillet with the lamb; simmer, covered, 15–20 minutes, stirring occasionally, until all ingredients are tender. Discard the yellow onion.

VARIATION:

- FOR A RICHER, ROBUST FLAVOR, ADD 1/2 CUP OF DRY RED WINE.

Low-Fat Option:

- REPLACE THE LAMB WITH CUBED CHICKEN OR TURKEY.

Desserts

Mango Pear Crisp

SERVES 4–6

The combination of mango and pears makes for a delightful treat for your taste buds.

3	pears, cored, peeled and sliced
3	mangoes, cored, peeled and sliced
2 tbsp	cornstarch
1 tbsp	brown sugar

TOPPING

1 cup	rolled oats
1/2 tsp	cinnamon
2 tbsp	brown sugar
1/2 tsp	vanilla
2 tbsp	pear nectar
1 tbsp	butter

In a mixing bowl combine the pears, mango, cornstarch and 1 tbsp brown sugar and mix well. For the topping, combine all ingredients in a food processor and process till moist. Place the pears and mango in a 9-inch pie plate and completely pack down with the topping. Bake at 375°F for 20 minutes or until brown.

Helen's Mango Cake

When I told my mother about our Caribbean trip, she became inspired. To my surprise, I received this cake shortly thereafter, which she sent air express, with a note attached: "Caribbean, huh? Try this one." She's right—and it's easy and delicious. Thanks, Mom!

3	eggs
1 cup	sugar
1/2 cup	vegetable oil
1 tsp	vanilla
1-1/2 cups	all-purpose flour
2 tsp	baking powder
Pinch	salt
2 cups	sliced mango (or any other fruit)
1/4 tsp	ground nutmeg

In a bowl with an electric beater beat the eggs, sugar, oil and vanilla for 3 minutes. Add the flour, baking powder and salt. Beat the mixture until smooth, about 1 minute. Pour batter into a 13- x 9-inch greased cake pan. Arrange the mango slices on top and sprinkle with nutmeg. Bake at 350°F for 30 minutes or until a toothpick inserted comes out clean.

VARIATION:

⊚ SUBSTITUTE ANY OTHER FRUIT FOR THE MANGO.

Rum Cake

Everyone on board the Century cruise ship was telling me that when I got to Grand Cayman I had to see a man named Anthony Lindley from the Wholesome Bakery Co. Ltd. So I did, and, boy, was I glad I did! They have the most delicious rum cake I have ever tasted. (Sorry, Mom!) Passengers were coming back on ship with large containers, or tins, of this Grand Cayman specialty. And here's the recipe. I know you'll agree with me.

1 lb	yellow cake mix
6 oz	vanilla pudding mix
1/2 cup	water
1/4 cup	dark rum
1/4 cup	vegetable oil
2	eggs, beaten

RUM SYRUP

3/4 cup	water
1/2 cup	brown sugar
1/4 cup	dark rum

In a large bowl gently fold together cake mix, pudding mix, water, rum, oil and eggs. Let stand for 2 minutes. Stir briskly until the batter is smooth. Pour batter into a well-greased Bundt pan or 9-inch cake pan. Bake at 400°F for 30 minutes or until toothpick when inserted comes out clean. Let cake cool slightly in pan on a rack. Meanwhile, in a small saucepan bring rum syrup ingredients to a boil, stirring until sugar is dissolved. Remove from heat. Remove warm cake from pan. Pour 3/4 cup of the rum syrup into the warm cake pan. Return the cake to the pan. Pour the remaining syrup over the cake. Let stand for 15 minutes, then remove cake from pan and let cool.

© *Recipe from the Wholesome Bakery Co. Ltd., Grand Cayman.*

Ken's Orange Rum Cake

This cake combines oranges with dark rum. I tasted a Puerto Rican version and was so impressed that I had to bring a whole cake back to the ship. Even the beseeching of my lovely co-host, Mary Jo, went ignored as I indulged my sweet tooth in solitary!

2 cups	all-purpose flour
1 tbsp	baking powder
1/2 tsp	salt
1/2 cup	butter, softened
1 cup	sugar
3	eggs
2 tbsp	finely chopped orange rind
1 tbsp	dark rum
1/2 tsp	vanilla
1/2 cup	freshly squeezed orange juice

Sift together the flour, baking powder and salt. In a bowl cream the butter and sugar. Beat in the eggs one at a time, beating well after each addition. Combine the orange rind, rum and vanilla. Mix in the dry ingredients alternately with the orange juice. Pour batter into a 9-inch cake pan or loaf pan and bake at 350°F for 50 minutes or until a toothpick inserted in the center comes out clean.

Pineapple Delight Cake

Hawaiian pineapples have dominated the world market so thoroughly that many people would probably be surprised to learn that this fruit was not even planted there until 1790, some three centuries after it was discovered by companions of Christopher Columbus on the Caribbean island of Guadeloupe. Another misconception is its genus—even Larousse mistakenly called it a large cultivated strawberry, when it is really a member of the bromelia family, known for its ability to hold water. Whatever its background, there is no mistaking the sweet succulence of the pineapple, and in this recipe my mother, Helen, has used it to perfection. You can certainly tell we ate well as kids!

BASE

2 cups	all-purpose flour
1 cup	brown sugar
1 cup	butter, softened
2 tsp	baking powder

FILLING

2 cans	crushed pineapple (19 oz/540 mL) OR 2 cups chopped fresh pineapple
2 tbsp	cornstarch
1 cup	sugar

TOPPING

2	eggs
1/2 cup	sugar
2 tsp	vanilla
1-1/2 cups	shredded sweetened coconut

VARIATION:

• REPLACE THE PINEAPPPLE WITH OTHER FRUIT.

BASE

In a large bowl mix the base ingredients. Press into a
13- x 9-inch cake pan.

FILLING

In a saucepan combine the filling ingredients. Simmer
and stir until thickened. Spread evenly over the cake
base.

TOPPING

Beat the eggs and sugar until light and frothy. Beat
in the vanilla. Stir in the coconut. Spread evenly over
the filling.

Bake at 325°F for 45 minutes or until golden.

Sautéed Coconut, Mango and Pear

SERVES 4

The origin of the coconut has never been established. Because it floats and takes root wherever it washes up, coconut migration has been impossible to trace. The best guess places its origin in the Indo-Malaysian region, where its importance as a principal food and mystic cultural object is unsurpassed. Remember that the next time you bite into a Bounty candy bar, though I'm sure Lieutenant Bligh would not be amused! It's not often you sauté a dessert, but try this one.

1 tsp	vegetable oil
2	mangoes, sliced
4	pears, peeled and sliced
1 tbsp	brown sugar
2 tbsp	shredded sweetened coconut
1/2 tsp	cinnamon
1 tbsp	dark rum
1 cup	whipped cream

In a sauté pan or skillet heat the oil. Sprinkle the mango and pears with the sugar, coconut and cinnamon. Sauté gently for 2 minutes, making sure the mango and pears stay slightly firm. Mix in rum. Serve with whipped cream.

VARIATIONS:

⊙ REPLACE THE WHIPPED CREAM WITH ICE CREAM.

⊙ REPLACE THE PEARS WITH APPLES.

Banana Coconut Loaf with Island Spices

The first bananas in America were planted on the island of Hispaniola by Friar Tomás de Berlanga in 1516, but it wasn't until after World War I that they became readily available throughout North America and Europe. In Helen's kitchen (that's my mom), a quite wonderful dessert was created when she combined the sweetness of the banana with the agreeably exotic essence of a coconut.

1-1/4 cups	all-purpose flour
2 tsp	baking powder
1 tsp	cinnamon
1/2 tsp	ground nutmeg
1/2 tsp	salt
1/4 tsp	baking soda
1/2 cup	shortening
1 cup	sugar
3	eggs
1 cup	mashed banana (about 2 large)
1 tsp	vanilla
1/2 cup	shredded sweetened coconut

Sift together twice the flour, baking powder, cinnamon, nutmeg, salt and baking soda. In a medium bowl mash the shortening with a fork and slowly add the sugar; beat in the eggs one at a time, mixing well after each addition. Beat in the dry ingredients, alternating with the bananas. Mix in the vanilla and coconut. Turn the batter into a greased medium-sized loaf pan. Bake at 350°F for 45 minutes or until a toothpick inserted in the center comes out clean.

Grilled Bananas with Brown Sugar

SERVES 4

The banana was eaten in the Indus valley more than four thousand years ago, but because it is perishable, and therefore hard to transport, its journey around the world was exceedingly slow. Now it is recognized, in its cultivated state, as a desirable fruit, finding its way into many recipes. The banana lends its delicate flavor to this dessert, which never fails to impress my dinner guests.

8	firm bananas (not too ripe)
2 tbsp	dark rum
2 tbsp	brown sugar
1 tsp	cinnamon
1 cup	crème fraîche or whipped cream
	Fresh mint, for garnish

Halve the bananas lengthwise. Brush rum on each side and grill 2–4 minutes to create grill marks. While grilling, evenly sprinkle with the brown sugar and cinnamon. Place four pieces on each dessert plate with crème fraîche in the center. Place a small piece of mint on top for garnish.

VARIATION:

- REPLACE WHIPPED CREAM WITH VANILLA ICE CREAM.

Pie de Margarita
MAKES ONE 9-INCH PIE

One bite of this pie and you will think you're in heaven. When I had a slice at the family-run Pancho's Backyard restaurant, in Cozumel, I wanted to bring the whole thing back with me—the texture and taste were out of this world. I managed to control myself that night, but couldn't wait to get home to my kitchen and try it myself. You'll see what I mean when you make it!

4	eggs, separated
2 cups	sugar
3/4 cup	lime juice
3 tbsp	white tequila
3 tbsp	orange liqueur
1 tbsp	unflavored gelatin
	Grated peel of half a lime
Pinch	Salt
1	baked 9-inch pie shell
	Thin lime slices, for garnish

In a blender blend the egg yolks, 1 cup of the sugar, lime juice, tequila, orange liqueur, gelatin, lime peel and salt until foamy. Chill for 10 minutes. Beat the egg whites until foamy; gradually beat in the remaining sugar. Fold egg yolk mixture into egg whites gently but thoroughly. Pour filling into pie shell, spreading evenly. Freeze for 1-1/2 hours, then chill in the refrigerator at least 1 hour. Garnish each serving with a slice of lime.

⊙ *Recipe from Pancho's Backyard Restaurant, Cozumel, Mexico.*

Key Lime Pie
MAKES ONE 9-INCH PIE

The charm of Key West is enhanced by its wonderful restaurants and food. Fresh in my memory are all the delightful experiences of Kelly's Caribbean Bar, Grill and Brewery—their annual Key West Jazz Festival, touring the historic edifice that is Kelly's (it was the first Pan Am ticket building), and the gracious owner of this concern, Kelly McGillis, star of **Top Gun** and **Witness**. Key lime pie is a must in Key West, and the best thus far is from this famous establishment.

4	eggs, separated
1 can	sweetened condensed milk (16 oz)
1/2 cup	Key lime juice
1 tsp	white or dark rum
1	baked 9-inch pie shell
1/2 tsp	cream of tartar
6 tbsp	sugar

Beat the egg yolks. Beat in the condensed milk, lime juice and rum until mixture is thick. Pour into the pie shell. In a separate bowl, beat egg whites until soft peaks form; gradually beat in cream of tartar and sugar until stiff peaks form. Spread meringue over filling. Bake at 350°F until meringue is golden brown, about 35 minutes.

○ *Recipe from Kelly's Caribbean Bar, Grill and Brewery, Key West.*

Chart House Mud Pie

MAKES ONE 9-INCH PIE

The Chart House Restaurant in San Juan, Puerto Rico, is beautifully located on a narrow isthmus that leads to Old San Juan. In an historic mansion, ensconced within the encircling verandas, nothing could be more delightful than coffee and a piece of their chilled Chart House Mud Pie. Ice cream lovers will go crazy for this gourmet dessert!

1 cup	chocolate wafers, crushed
1/2 cup	butter, melted
1 gallon	coffee ice cream, softened
1-1/4 cups	cold fudge sauce
	Sliced almonds
	Whipped cream

Stir together crushed chocolate wafers and butter. Press mixture into a 9-inch pie plate. Fill pie shell with coffee ice cream. Top with fudge sauce. Freeze for at least 10 hours. Serve pie on chilled dessert plates, topped with whipped cream and sliced almonds.

Recipe from the Chart House Restaurant, San Juan, Puerto Rico.

Grand Cayman Coconut and Rice Krispie Square

The Grand Cayman Coconut and Rice Krispie Square is one of my favorite desserts. I love this recipe because it takes no time to prepare and you can add other ingredients to have it match the rest of your dinner menu. Occasionally, I add fresh fruit like strawberries or apples and applesauce. Experiment!

1/4 cup	unsalted butter
45	regular-size marshmallows
1/2 tsp	vanilla
1/4 tsp	cinnamon
1 cup	shredded sweetened coconut
1 tsp	dark rum (optional)
5 cups	Rice Krispies cereal

In a large saucepan or soup pot melt the butter on low heat; add the marshmallows. Stir until marshmallows are melted and mixture is blended well. Add the vanilla, cinnamon, shredded coconut and dark rum (if using). Mix well. Mix in Rice Krispies, one cup at a time. Mix well and then press into a greased or nonstick 13- x 9-inch cake pan. Chill for an hour before cutting into squares.

VARIATION:

◎ REPLACE PLAIN MARSHMALLOWS WITH FLAVORED ONES.

Tropical Drinks

Ken's Banana Rum Shake

SERVES 4

The banana has never been truly appreciated for its culinary possibilities, yet beyond the rather homely appearance lies a fleshy, deliciously sweet fruit with limits only in your own imagination. And so I've combined it with a few of my other favorite ingredients to bring you another liquid entertainment. A word of caution: this one goes down so smoothly, you'll forget there's alcohol in it!

12	ice cubes
2	bananas
2 cups	orange juice
1 cup	yogurt
1/2 cup	dark rum
2 tbsp	brown sugar
1/2 tsp	vanilla
2 tbsp	sweetened coconut

In a blender blend all the ingredients until frothy.

VARIATION:

◎ REPLACE YOGURT WITH VANILLA ICE CREAM (YUM-YUM).

Low-Fat Option:

◎ USE LOW-FAT OR NON-FAT YOGURT.

Health Option:

◎ REPLACE SUGAR WITH CALORIE-REDUCED LIQUID SWEETENER.

Ken's Orange Juice Swizzler

SERVES 4

In ancient China, cinnamon was known as kwei. It is actually the inner bark of a laurel-like evergreen tree. I have used its fragrant sweetness in my Orange Juice Swizzler to complement the richness of the other ingredients. This fluid treat takes no time at all to prepare yet will delight even the most discerning taste bud!

12	ice cubes
4 cups	orange juice
1/2 cup	dark rum
2 tbsp	orange rind
2 tbsp	brown sugar
2 tbsp	lemon juice
1/2 tsp	vanilla
1/2 tsp	cinnamon

In a blender blend all the ingredients. (You may have to do this in 2 batches.) Serve immediately or chill before serving.

VARIATION:

◉ REPLACE THE DARK RUM WITH LIGHT RUM.

Mexican Wine Spritzer

My Mexican Wine Spritzer is a refreshing blend of flavors result-
ing in a different drink that sparkles—in your glass and on your
taste buds! Although this drink contains alcohol, its strength is
sufficiently diluted to allow for seconds.

1 bottle	dry red wine (750 mL)
1 bottle	carbonated water (750 mL)
1 cup	cranberry juice
1 cup	orange juice
1/2 cup	thinly sliced strawberries
2 tbsp	sugar
1 tsp	orange rind
1	orange, thinly sliced

In a large pitcher combine all the ingredients. Chill
1 hour before serving.

VARIATION:

⊚ REPLACE RED WINE
   WITH WHITE WINE.

Puerto Rican Fruit Punch

Punch was first made in India with five ingredients only: spirits, tea, sugar, fruit juice and water. Thankfully, we have experimented over the years, and the results are as varied as the individuals who create them. My mixture includes citrus fruit and cinnamon, flavorings that have an affinity for alcohol. And you get to use up your leftover fruit.

12	ice cubes
2 cups	pineapple juice
2 cups	orange juice
2 cups	peach nectar
1 cup	cranberry juice
1/2 cup	pineapple chunks
1/2 cup	sliced strawberries
1/2 cup	dark rum
1/2 tsp	ground nutmeg
1/2 tsp	cinnamon
2	peaches, sliced
1	orange, thinly sliced

In a large punch bowl combine the ingredients. Chill 1 hour before serving.

Strawberry Daiquiri
SERVES 4

Almost any part of a plant—seeds, leaves, roots, fruit and kernels—can be macerated with or infused in alcohol to give a spirited flavoring. The spirit we get when sugarcane is fermented or distilled is that light colorless essence called rum. White rum is traditional for tropical drinks, but you can use either dark or light rum in this strawberry daiquiri recipe. Don't forget the little bamboo umbrella—I'm convinced it magically enhances the moment.

12	ice cubes
1 cup	strawberries
1 cup	cranberry juice
1/4 cup	rum
2 tbsp	lemon juice
1 tbsp	sugar

In a blender blend all the ingredients until frothy. This drink must be served with one of those bamboo umbrellas.

VARIATION:

⊙ REPLACE THE STRAWBERRIES WITH MANGO.

Piña Colada

SERVES 4

Being at sea is one of the most pleasurable parts of a cruise, and
I couldn't think of a better way to while away the afternoon than to
lounge in the warm sunshine sipping a tall, cold drink—a piña
colada, to be exact. In fact, to my surprise, I noticed so many piña
coladas being served that I lost count. (How could you doubt me?
Of course I tried to count them all!) Try this one at home, but watch
out—it has a kick!

12	ice cubes
2 cups	pineapple juice
1 cup	crushed pineapple
1 cup	sweetened coconut milk
1/2 cup	dark rum
1 tbsp	lemon juice
1/2 tsp	vanilla (optional)
1/4 tsp	cinnamon OR 4 cinnamon sticks as stir sticks

In a blender blend all the ingredients until frothy. Serve
immediately with bamboo umbrellas.

Virgin Piña Colada
SERVES 4

Pineapple is a hardy perennial plant with a high sugar content and a firm flesh that hints of apple, strawberry and peach all at once. It adds its traditional sweetness to my non-alcoholic version of the piña colada. This is a delightful alternative for people who are allergic to alcohol—like me.

12	ice cubes
2 cups	crushed pineapple
2 cups	pineapple juice
1 cup	sweetened coconut milk
6	maraschino cherries
1/2 tsp	vanilla
1/4 tsp	cinnamon

In a blender blend the ingredients until frothy.

Papaya and Mango Shake (Non-Alcoholic)

SERVES 4

The magic of yogurt has been passed from one generation to the next for countless years. History recounts that King Francois I, suffering from a persistent intestinal complaint, sent for a Jewish doctor from Constantinople who was reputed to have developed a cure for just such an ailment using yogurt. The doctor did, in fact, set right his royal client. After shooting **What's for Dinner?** on location in Ocho Rios, we refreshed ourselves with a Papaya and Mango Shake.

6	ice cubes
4 cups	orange juice
1 cup	sliced mango
1 cup	sliced papaya
1 cup	yogurt
2 tbsp	brown sugar
1/4 tsp	ground nutmeg
1/2 tsp	vanilla

In a blender blend the ingredients until smooth. Serve immediately or freeze for 10 minutes.

VARIATION:

⊙ REPLACE YOGURT WITH VANILLA ICE CREAM (YUM).

Low-Fat Option:

⊙ USE NON-FAT YOGURT.

Health Option:

⊙ USE A CALORIE-REDUCED LIQUID SWEETENER INSTEAD OF BROWN SUGAR.

Sangria (Non-Alcoholic)

Sangria is a popular wine-based drink usually made by adding
sugar and ice to Spanish red wine. Successful variations of this
liquid pleasure are making their way around the world. A little
Calypso music, a warm summer night, Sangria in hand—and
you're transported to a tropical paradise!

1 bottle	non-alcoholic red wine (750 mL)
1 cup	orange juice
1 cup	cranberry juice
1/2 cup	sliced strawberries
1 tbsp	lemon juice
1	orange, thinly sliced

In a large pitcher combine all the ingredients. Chill at
least 1 hour before serving.

Fruit Punch (Non-Alcoholic)

Punch was originally made in India with locally produced spirits. The custom was to use five ingredients and the Indian word for five was "panch"—thus in English we get "punch." Punches are festive and flavorful, and this non-alcoholic version uses a traditionally taste-bud-tingling variety of five fruits!

2 cups	orange juice
2 cups	pineapple juice
2 cups	cranberry juice
1/2 cup	small pineapple pieces
1/2 cup	sliced strawberries
1 tbsp	orange rind

In a large pitcher combine all the ingredients. Chill for 1 hour. Add ice as needed to keep the punch cool.

VARIATION:

○ REPLACE ANY OF THE JUICES WITH APPLE, GRAPE, MANGO OR PEAR JUICE.

Grapefruit Sunrise

SERVES 4

Chilled grapefruit juice is an excellent appetite-whetter, as we in North America discovered from the Chinese, who eat the fruit at the beginning of a meal. My Grapefruit Sunrise is a big hit at my brunches.

12	ice cubes
4 cups	freshly squeezed grapefruit juice
2 cups	orange juice
2 tbsp	brown sugar
1 tsp	orange rind
1/2	grapefruit, peeled

In a blender blend all the ingredients until frothy. (You may have to do this in 2 batches.) Transfer to a large pitcher and stir occasionally with a wooden spoon.

VARIATION:

⊚ REPLACE THE GRAPE-FRUIT WITH ALL ORANGE.

Low-Fat Option:

⊚ REPLACE BROWN SUGAR WITH CALORIE-REDUCED LIQUID SWEETENER.

Index

Butternut Squash Soup with Cinnamon, 44
Calypso Herbed Eggplant Cutlet, 94
Basic Pizza, 68
Caribbean Vegetable Stew, 87
Carrot and Ginger Soup, 42
Chiles Rellenos, 21
Chilled Apple Soup, 36
Chilled Banana-Pineapple-Coconut Soup, 34
Chilled Peach Soup with Mint, 35
Chilled Pear and Apple Soup with Coconut, 37
Chilled Strawberry Soup, 38
Deep-Dish Vegetable Pizza on Focaccia, 72
Focaccia Fingers, 19
Grilled Portobello Mushrooms with Penne, 93
Guacamole, 18
Island Medley of Vegetables, 86
Ken's Egg Zucchini Pie, 89
Ken's Favorite Fruit Salad, 56
Low-Fat Caribbean Coleslaw, 55
Mexican Black Bean Soup with Salsa and
   Corn, 41
Mexican Pepper and Avocado Salad, 57
Mexican Pita, 76
Mexican Vegetables Fajitas, 96
Mexican Vegetarian Chili, 90
Mexican Veggie Pizza, 71
Mezclun with Chèvre and Mango Vinaigrette,
   54

Pasta Salad with Caribbean Fruit and
   Vegetables, 58
   Penne with Grilled Vegetables, 79
   Sesame Grilled Portobello Mushrooms, 92
   Sesame Grilled Vegetable Salad with Asiago
      Cheese, 59
   Sesame Tofu Cubes, 20
   Spicy Tofu Balls, 98
   Sweet Red Pepper Soup, 43
   Tofu Stir-Fry with Spicy Tomatoes and
      Ginger, 100
   Vegetable and Tofu Brochettes, 101
   Vegetable Chow Mein, 97
   Vegetarian Bean Stew, 88
   Vegetarian "Rajas" Pizza, 70
   West Indian Vegetable Stew, 84
Vegetarian "Rajas" Pizza, 70
Virgin Piña Colada, 184

Watercress
   Cold Beef and Orange Salad on Watercress, 63
   West Indian Vegetable Stew, 84
   Wholesome Bakery Co. Ltd., 166

Yucatan Beef Stew, 149

Zucchini
   Ken's Egg Zucchini Pie, 89

If you'd like to write to Ken Kostick, please address your letters to:

Ken Kostick
Box 116
2255 Queen Street East
Toronto, Ontario
M4E 1G3